Selections from the

World's Devotional Classics

Volume X

Woolman to Matheson

𝕬𝖚𝖌𝖚𝖘𝖙 𝕿𝖍𝖔𝖑𝖚𝖈𝖐

Selections
from the
World's Devotional Classics

EDITED BY

Robert Scott and George W. Gilmore
Editors of The Homiletic Review

IN TEN VOLUMES

Volume X
Wollman to Matheson

FUNK & WAGNALLS COMPANY
NEW YORK AND LONDON

Contents Volume Ten

Selections

Prayers

Contents

SELECTIONS FROM

The Writings

OF

JOHN WOOLMAN

Introduction

JOHN WOOLMAN

American Quaker preacher and reformer, was born in Northampton, Burlington County, N. J., August, 1720; died at York, England, October 7, 1772. In early life he was a clerk in a store and opened a school for poor children. Afterward he learned tailoring in order to support himself while traveling from place to place. Much of his time was given to writing and speaking against slavery. He is best known by his "Journal" (1775). He also wrote "Some Considerations on the Keeping of Negroes" (1754, part 2, 1762); "Considerations on Pure Wisdom and Human Policy, on Labor, on Schools, and on the Right Use of the Lord's Outward Gifts" (1768); Considerations on the True Harmony of Mankind, and How it is to be Maintained" (1770); and "A Word of Remembrance and Caution to the Rich" (1793).

Introduction

My mind hath often been affected with sorrow, on account of the prevailing of that spirit, which leads from an humble waiting on the inward teaching of Christ, to pursue ways of living attended with unnecessary labor, and which draws from the minds of many people to seek after outward power and to strive for riches, which frequently introduce oppression and bring forth wars and grievous calamities.

It is with reverence that I acknowledge the mercies of our heavenly Father, who in infinite love did visit me in my youth, and wrought a belief in me that through true obedience a state of inward purity may be known in this life, in which we may love mankind in the same love with which our redeemer loveth us, and therein learn resignation to endure hardships, for the real good of others.

"While the eye is single, the whole body is full of light" (Matt. 6:22), but for want of this, selfish desires and an imaginary superiority darken the mind; hence injustice frequently proceeds; and where this is the case, to convince the judgment is the most effectual remedy.

Where violent measures are pursued in opposing injustice, the passions and resentments of the injured frequently operate in the prosecution of their designs; and after conflicts productive of very great calamities, the minds of contending parties often remain as little acquainted with the pure principle of divine love as they were before; but where people walk in that pure light in which all their "works are wrought in God" (John 3:21), and under oppression persevere in the meek spirit and abide firm in the cause of truth, without actively complying with oppressive demands, through those the Lord hath often manifested his power, in opening the understandings of others, to the promoting righteousness in the earth.

A time, I believe, is coming wherein this divine work will so spread and prevail, that "nation shall not lift up sword against nation, nor learn war any more" (Isa. 2:4). And as we, through the tender mercies of God, do feel that this precious work is begun, I am concerned to encourage my brethren and sisters in a holy care and diligence, that each of us may so live, under the sanctifying power of truth, as to be redeemed from all unnecessary cares; that our eye being single to him, no customs, however prevalent, which are contrary to the wisdom from above, may hinder us from faithfully following his holy leadings in whatsoever he may graciously appoint for us.

Considerations On Pure Wisdom and Human Policy

To have our trust settled in the Lord, and not to seek after nor desire outward treasures any further than his Holy Spirit leads us therein, is a happy state, as saith the prophet, "Blessed is the man that trusteth in the Lord, and whose hope the Lord is."

Pure wisdom leads people into lowliness of mind, in which they learn resignation to the divine will and contentment in suffering for his cause, when they can not keep a clear conscience without suffering. In this pure wisdom the mind is attentive to the root and original spring of motions and desires; and as we know the Lord to be our refuge, and find no safety but in humbly walking before him, we feel an holy engagement that every desire which leads therefrom may be brought to judgment.

While we proceed in this precious way, and find ardent longings for a full deliverance from every thing which defiles, all prospects of gain that are not consistent with the wisdom from above are considered as snares, and an inward concern is felt that we may live under the cross, and faithfully attend to that Holy Spirit which is sufficient to preserve out of them.

When I have considered that saying of Christ (Matt. 6:19), "Lay not up for yourselves treasures upon earth," his omnipotence hath often occurred to my mind.

While we believe that he is everywhere present with his people, and that perfect goodness, wisdom, and power are united in him, how comfortable is the consideration.

Our wants may be great, but his power is greater. We may be opprest and despised, but he is able to turn our patient sufferings into profit to ourselves and to the advancement of his work on earth. His people, who feel the power of his cross to crucify all that is selfish in them, who are engaged in outward concerns from a convincement that it is their duty, and resign themselves and their treasures to him; these feel that it is dangerous to give way to that in us which craves riches and greatness in this world.

As the heart truly contrite earnestly desires "to know Christ, and the fellowship of his sufferings" (Phil. 3:10), so far as the Lord for gracious ends may lead into them;

as such feel that it is their interest to put their trust in God, and to seek no gain but that which he by his Holy Spirit leads into; so, on the contrary, they who do not reverently wait for this divine Teacher, and are not humbly concerned according to their measure "to fill up that which is behind of the afflictions of Christ" (Col. 1:24), in patiently suffering for the promoting righteousness in the earth; but have an eye toward the power of men and the outward advantage of wealth, these are often attentive to those employments which appear profitable, even tho the gains arise from such trade and business which proceeds from the workings of that spirit which is estranged from the self-denying life of an humble, contrite Christian.

While I write on this subject, I feel my mind tenderly affected toward those honestly disposed people who have been brought up in employments attended with those difficulties. To such I may say, in the feeling of our Heavenly Father's love, and number myself with you, O that our eyes may be single to the Lord! May we reverently wait on him for strength, to lay aside all unnecessary expense of every kind, and learn contentment in a plain, simple life. May we in lowliness submit to the leadings of his Spirit, and enter upon any outward employ which he graciously points out to us, and then whatever difficulties arise in consequence of our faithfulness, I trust they will work for our good.

Small treasure to a resigned mind is sufficient. How happy is it to be content with a little, to live in humility, and feel that in us which breathes out this language, Abba! Father!

If that called the wisdom of this world had no resemblance of true wisdom, the name of wisdom, I suppose, had not been given to it.

As wasting outward substance to gratify vain desires, on one hand, so slothfulness and neglect, on the other, do often involve men and their families in trouble, and reduce them to want and distress; to shun both these opposite vices is good in itself and hath a resemblance of wisdom; but while people thus provident have it principally in view to get riches and power and the friendship of this world, and do not humbly wait for the Spirit of truth to lead them into purity; these through an anxious care to obtain the end desired, reach forth for gain in worldly wisdom and, in regard to their inward state, fall into divers temptations and snares. And tho such may think of applying wealth to good purposes and to use their power to prevent oppression, yet wealth and power is often applied otherwise; nor can we depart from the leadings of our holy Shepherd without going into confusion.

Great wealth is frequently attended with power, which nothing but divine love can qualify the mind to use rightly; and as to the humility and uprightness of our children after us, how great is the uncertainty! If in acquiring wealth we take hold on the wisdom which is from beneath, and depart from the leadings of truth, and example our children herein, we have great cause to apprehend that wealth may be a snare to them, and prove an injury to others over whom their wealth may give them power.

To be redeemed from that wisdom which is from beneath, and walk in the light of the Lord, is a precious situation; thus his people are brought to put their trust in him; and in this humble confidence in his wisdom, goodness, and power, the righteous find a refuge in adversities superior to the greatest outward helps, and a comfort more certain than any worldly advantages can afford.

On Schools

[Suffer the little children to come unto me, and forbid them not, for of such is the kingdom of God.—Mark 10:14.]

To encourage children to do things with a view to get praise of men to me appears an obstruction to their being inwardly acquainted with the Spirit of truth. For it is the work of the Holy Spirit to direct the mind to God, that in all our proceedings we may have a single eye to him—to give alms in secret, to fast in secret, and labor to keep clear of that disposition reproved by our Savior, "All their works which they do is for to be seen of men" (Matt. 23:5).

That divine light which enlightens all men, I believe, does often shine in the minds of children very early; and to humbly wait for wisdom, that our conduct toward them may tend to forward their acquaintance with it, and strengthen them in obedience thereto, appears to me to be a duty on all of us. By cherishing the spirit of pride and the love of praise in them, I believe they may sometimes improve faster in learning than otherwise they would; but to take measures to forward children in learning which naturally tend to divert their minds from true humility appears to me to savor of the wisdom of this world.

If tutors are not acquainted with sanctification of spirit, nor experienced in an humble waiting for the leadings of truth, but follow the maxims of the wisdom of this world, such children who are under their tuition appear to me to be in danger of imbibing thoughts and apprehensions reverse to that meekness and lowliness of heart which is necessary for all the true followers of Christ.

Children at an age fit for schools are in a time of life which requires the patient attention of pious people, and if we commit them to the tuition of such, whose minds we believe are not rightly prepared to "train them up in the nurture and admonition of the Lord," we are in danger of not acting the part of faithful parents toward them; for our Heavenly Father doth not require us to do evil that good may come of it; and it is needful that we deeply examine ourselves, lest we get entangled in the wisdom of this world, and through wrong apprehensions take such methods in education as may prove a great injury to the minds of our children.

It is a lovely sight to behold innocent children; and when they are sent to such schools where their tender minds are in imminent danger of being led astray by tutors who do not live a self-denying life, or by the conversation of such children who do not live in innocence, it is a case much to be lamented.

While a pious tutor hath the charge of no more children than he can take due care of, and keeps his authority in the truth, the good spirit in which he leads and governs works on the minds of such who are not hardened, and his labors not only tend to bring them forward in outward learning, but to open their understandings with respect to the true Christian life; but where a person hath charge of too many, and his thoughts and time are so much employed in the outward affairs of his school that he does not so weightily attend to the spirit and conduct of each individual as to be enabled to administer rightly to all in due season; through such omission he not only suffers as to the state of his own mind, but the minds of the children are in danger of suffering also.

To watch the spirit of children, to nurture them in gospel love, and labor to help them against that which would mar the beauty of their minds, is a debt we owe them; and a faithful performance of our duty not only tends to their lasting benefit and our own peace, but also to render their company agreeable to us.

Instruction, thus administered, reaches the pure witness in the minds of such children who are not hardened, and begets love in them toward those who thus lead them on; but where too great a number are committed to a tutor, and he through much cumber omits a careful attention to the minds of children, there is danger of disorders gradually increasing among them, till the effects thereof appear in their conduct too strong to be easily remedied.

A care hath lived on my mind, that more time might be employed by parents at home, and by tutors at school, in weightily attending to the spirit and inclinations of children, and that we may so lead, instruct, and govern them in this tender part of life that nothing may be omitted in our power to help them on their way to become the children of our Father who is in heaven.

Meditating on the situation of schools in our provinces, my mind hath at times been affected with sorrow, and under these exercises it hath appeared to me that if those who have large estates were faithful stewards, and laid no rent nor interest nor other demands higher than is consistent with universal love; and those in lower circumstances would, under a moderate employ, shun unnecessary expense, even to the smallest article; and all unite in humbly seeking to the Lord, he would graciously instruct us and strengthen us to relieve the youth from various snares in which many of them are entangled.

On the Right Use of the Lord's Outward Gifts

As our understandings are opened by the pure light, we experience that, through an inward approaching to God, the mind is strengthened in obedience; and that by gratifying those desires which are not of his begetting those approaches to him are obstructed, and the deceivable spirit gains strength.

These truths, being as it were engraven upon our hearts, and our everlasting interest in Christ evidently concerned herein, we become fervently engaged that nothing may be nourished which tends to feed pride or self-love in us. Thus in pure obedience we are not only instructed in our duty to God, but also in the affairs which necessarily relate to this life, and the Spirit of truth which guides into all truth leavens the mind with a pious concern, that "whatsoever we do in word or deed, may be done in his name" (Col. 3:17).

Hence such buildings, furniture, food, and raiment as best answer our necessities, and are the least likely to feed that selfish spirit which is our enemy, are the most acceptable to us. In this state the mind is tender and inwardly watchful, that the love of gain draw us not into any business which may weaken our

14

love to our Heavenly Father or bring unnecessary trouble to any of his creatures.

Thus the way gradually opens to cease from that spirit which craves riches and things fetched far, which so mixeth with the customs of this world, and so intrudes upon the true harmony of life, that the right medium of labor is very much departed from. And as the minds of people are settled in a steady concern not to hold nor possess any thing but what may be held consistent with the wisdom from above, they consider what they possess as the gift of God, and are inwardly exercised that in all parts of their conduct they may act agreeable to the nature of the peaceable government of Christ.

A little supports such a life; and in a state truly resigned to the Lord the eye is single to see what outward employ he leads into as a means of our subsistence, and a lively care is maintained to hold to that without launching further.

There is a harmony in the several parts of this divine work in the hearts of people; he who leads them to cease from those gainful employments, carried on in that wisdom which is from beneath, delivers also from the desire after worldly greatness, and reconciles the mind to a life so plain that a little doth suffice. Here the real comforts of life are not lessened. Moderate exercise in the way of true wisdom is pleasant to mind and body. Food and raiment sufficient, tho in the greatest simplicity, is accepted with content and gratitude.

The mutual love subsisting between the faithful followers of Christ is more pure than that friendship which is not seasoned with humility, how specious soever the appearance.

Where people depart from pure wisdom in one case, it is often the introduction to depart from it in many more; and thus a spirit which seeks for outward greatness, and leads into worldly wisdom to attain it and support it, gets possession of the mind.

In beholding the customary departure from the true medium of labor, and that unnecessary toil which many go through in supporting outward greatness and procuring delicacies; in beholding how the true calmness of life is changed into hurry, and that many, by eagerly pursuing outward treasure, are in great danger of withering as to the inward state of the mind; in meditating on the works of this spirit, and on the desolations it makes among the professors of Christianity, I may thankfully acknowledge that I often feel pure love beget longings in my heart for the exaltation of the peaceable kingdom of Christ, and an engagement to labor according to the gift bestowed on me for the promoting an humble, plain, temperate way of living—a life where no unnecessary care nor expenses may encumber our minds, nor lessen our ability to do good; where no desires after riches or greatness may lead into hard dealing; where no connections with worldly-minded men may abate our love to God, nor weaken a true zeal for righteousness; a life wherein we may diligently labor for resignedness to do and suffer whatever our Heavenly Father may allot for us, in reconciling the world to himself.

When the Prophet Isaiah had uttered his vision, and declared that a time was coming wherein "swords should be beat into plowshares, and spears into pruning hooks, and that nation shall not lift up sword against nation, nor learn war any more," he immediately directs the minds of people to the divine teacher in this remarkable language, "O house of Jacob! come ye, and let us walk in the light of the Lord" (Isa. 2:5).

To wait for the direction of this light in all temporal as well as spiritual concerns appears necessary; for if in any case we enter lightly into temporal affairs without feeling this Spirit of Truth to open our way therein, and through the love of this world proceed on and seek for gain by that business or traffic which "is not of the Father, but of the world" (1 John 2:16), we fail in our testimony to the purity and peace of his government, and get into that which is for chastisement.

This matter hath lain heavy on my mind, it being evident that a life less humble, less simple and plain, than that which Christ leads his sheep into does necessarily require a support which pure wisdom does not provide for; hence there is no probability of our being "a peculiar people, so zealous of good works as to have no fellowship with works of darkness" (Titus 2: 14; Eph. 5: 11), while we have wants to supply which have their foundation in custom and do not come within the meaning of those expressions, "your Heavenly Father knoweth that ye have need of all these things" (Matt. 6: 32).

These things which he beholds necessary for his people, he fails not to give them in his own way and time; but as his ways are above our ways, and his thoughts above thoughts, so imaginary wants are different from these things which he knoweth that we have need of.

As my meditations have been on these things, compassion hath filled my heart toward my fellow creatures, involved in customs, grown up in the wisdom of this world, which is foolishness with God (1 Cor. 3: 19). And O that the youth may be so thoroughly experienced in an humble walking before the Lord, that they may be his children, and know him to be their refuge, their safe unfailing refuge, through the various dangers attending this uncertain state of being!

If those whose minds are redeemed from the love of wealth, and who are content with a plain, simple way of living, do yet find that to conduct the affairs of a family, without giving countenance to unrighteous proceedings, or having fellowship with works of darkness, the most diligent care is necessary.

If customs, distinguishable from universal righteousness, and opposite to the true self-denying life, are now prevalent, and so mixed with trade, and with almost every employ, that it is only through humble waiting on the inward guidance of truth, that we may reasonably hope to walk safely, and support an uniform testimony to the peaceable government of Christ:

If this be the case, how lamentably do they expose themselves to temptations, who give way to the love of riches, conform to expensive living, and reach forth for gain, to support customs, which our holy Shepherd leads not into.

Considerations On the True Harmony of Mankind and How Is It to Be Maintained

[And the Remnant of Jacob shall be in the midst of many People, as the Dew from the Lord, as the Showers upon the Grass, that tarrieth not for Man, nor waiteth for the Sons of Men.—Micah 5 : 7.]

Introduction

As mankind from one parent are divided into many families, and as trading to sea is greatly increased within a few ages past; amidst this extended commerce how necessary is it that the profest followers of Christ keep sacred his holy name, and be employed about trade and traffic no farther than justice and equity evidently accompanies? That we may give no just cause of offense to any, however distant or unable to plead their own cause; and may continually keep in view the spreading of the true and saving knowledge of God and his Son Jesus Christ among our fellow creatures, which through his infinite love some feel to be more precious than any other treasure.

John Woolman

I

On Serving the Lord In Our Outward Employments

Under the humbling dispensations of the Father of Mercies, I have felt an inward labor for the good of my fellow creatures, and a concern that the Holy Spirit, which alone can restore mankind to a state of true harmony, may with singleness of heart be waited for and followed. I trust there are many under that visitation, which if faithfully attended to will make them quick of understanding in the fear of the Lord, and qualify with firmness to be true patterns of the Christian life, who in living and walking may hold forth an invitation to others to come out of the entanglements of the spirit of this world.

And that which I feel first to express is a care for those who are in circumstances which appear difficult with respect to supporting their families in a way answerable to pure wisdom, that they may not be discouraged, but remember that in humbly obeying the leadings of Christ, he owneth us as his friends, "Ye are my friends if ye do whatsoever I command you"; and to be a friend to Christ is to be united to him who hath all power in heaven and in earth; and tho a woman may forget her sucking child, yet will he not forget his faithful ones.

The condition of many who dwell in cities hath often affected me with a brotherly sympathy, attended with a desire that resignation may be labored for; and where the Holy Leader directeth to a country life or some change of employ, he may be faithfully followed; for, under the refining hand of the Lord, I have seen that the inhabitants of some cities are greatly increased through some branches of business which the Holy Spirit doth not lead into, and that being entangled in these things tends to bring a cloud over the minds of people convinced of the leadings of this Holy Leader, and obstructs the coming of the kingdom of Christ on earth as it is in heaven.

Now if we indulge a desire to imitate our neighbors in those things which harmonize not with the true Christian walking, these entanglements may hold fast to us, and some who, in an awakening time, feel tender scruples with respect to their manner of life, may look on the example of others more noted in the church, who yet may not be refined from every degree of dross; and by looking on these examples, and desiring to support their families in a way pleasant to the natural mind, there may be danger of the worldly wisdom gaining strength in them, and of their departure from that pure feeling of truth which, if faithfully attended to, would teach contentment in the divine will, even in a very low estate.

One formerly speaking on the profitableness of true humility saith, "He that troubles not himself with anxious thoughts for more than is necessary, lives little less than the life of angels, whilst by a mind content with little he imitates their want of nothing" (Cave's "Primitive Christianity"). "It is not enough," says Tertullian, "that a Christian be chaste and modest, but he must appear to be so: a virtue of which he should have so great a store that it should flow from his mind upon his habit, and break from the retirements of his conscience, into the superficies of his life." "The garments we wear," says Clement, "ought to be mean and frugal—that is true simplicity of habit which takes away what is vain and superfluous, and that the best and most solid garment which is the farthest from curiosity."

Tho the change from day to night is by a motion so gradual as scarcely to be perceived, yet when night is come we behold it very different from the day; and thus as people become wise in their own eyes and prudent in their own sight, customs rise up from the spirit of this world, and spread by little and little, till a departure from the simplicity that there is in Christ becomes as distinguishable as light from darkness to such who are crucified to the world.

Our holy Shepherd, to encourage his flock in firmness and perseverance, reminds them of his love for them; "As the Father hath loved me, so have I loved you; continue ye in my love." And in another place graciously points out the danger of departing therefrom, by going into unsuitable employments; this he represents in the similitude of offense from that useful active member, the hand; and to fix the instruction the deeper, names the right hand; "If thy right hand offend thee, cut it off and cast it from thee." If thou feelest offense in thy employment, humbly follow him who leads into all truth, and is a strong and faithful friend to those who are resigned to him.

Again, he points out those things which, appearing pleasant to the natural mind, are not best for us, in the similitude of offense from the eye; "If thy right eye offend thee, pluck it out and cast it from thee." To pluck out the eye or cut off the hand is attended with sharp pain; and how precious is the instruction which our redeemer thus opens to us, that we may not faint under the most painful trial, but put our trust in him, even in him who sent an angel to feed Elijah in the wilderness;

who fed a multitude with a few barley loaves, and is now as attentive to the wants of his people as ever.

The Prophet Isaiah represents the unrighteous doings of the Israelites toward the poor as the fruits of an effeminate life; "As for my people, children are their oppressors, and women rule over them. What mean ye, that ye beat my people to pieces, and grind the faces of the poor? saith the Lord God." Then he mentions the haughtiness of the daughters of Sion, and enumerates many ornaments as instances of their vanity; to uphold which the poor were so hardly dealt with that he sets forth their poverty, their leanness and inability to help themselves, in the similitude of a man maimed by violence or beaten to pieces, and forced to endure the painful operation of having his face gradually worn away in the manner of grinding.

And I may here add, that at times, when I have felt true love open my heart toward my fellow creatures, and being engaged in weighty conversation in the cause of righteousness, the instructions I have received under these exercises in regard to the true use of the outward gifts of God have made deep and lasting impressions on my mind. I have here beheld how the desire to provide wealth and to uphold a delicate life hath grievously entangled many, and been like snares to their offspring; and tho some have been affected with a sense of their difficulties, and appeared desirous at times to be helped out of them; yet for want of abiding under the humbling power of truth they have continued in these entanglements; for in remaining conformable to this world, and giving way to a delicate life, this expensive way of living in parents and in children hath called for a large supply, and in answering this call the faces of the poor have been ground away and made thin through hard dealing.

There is balm, there is a physician; and O what longings do I feel! that we may embrace the means appointed for our healing, know that removed which now ministers cause for the cries of many people to ascend to heaven against their oppressors, and that we may see the true harmony restored.

"Behold how good and how pleasant it is, for brethren to dwell together in unity." The nature of this unity is thus opened by the apostle: "If we walk in the light, as Christ is in the light, we shall have fellowship one with another, and the blood of Christ will cleanse us from all sin."

The land may be polluted with innocent blood, which like the blood of Abel may cry to the Almighty; but those who "walk in the light, as Christ is in the light," they know the "Lamb of God, who taketh away sin."

Walking is a phrase frequently used in scripture to represent our journey through life, and appears to comprehend the various affairs and transactions properly relating to our being in this world.

Christ being the light, dwells always in the light; and if our walking be thus, and in every affair and concern we faithfully follow this divine leader, he preserves from giving just cause for any to quarrel with us. And where this foundation is laid and mutually kept to by families conversant with each other, the way is open for these comforts in society which our Heavenly Father intends as a part of our happiness in this world; and then we may experience the goodness and pleasantness of dwelling together in unity. But where ways of living take place which tend to oppression, and in the pursuit of wealth people do that to others which they know would not be acceptable to themselves, either in exercising an absolute power over them or otherwise laying on them unequitable burdens; here a fear lest that measure should be meted to them which they have measured to others incites a care to support that by craft and cunning devices which stands not on the firm foundation of righteousness. Thus the harmony of society is broken, and from hence commotions and wars do frequently arise in the world.

"Come out of Babylon, my people, that ye be not partakers of her sins, and that ye receive not of her plagues" (Rev. 15 : 3, 4). This Babel, or Babylon, was built in the spirit of self-exaltation: "Let us build us a city and a tower, whose top may reach to heaven, and let us make us a name" (Gen. 11 : 4). In departing from an humble trust in God and following a selfish spirit people have intentions to get the upper hand of their fellow creatures, privately meditate on means to obtain their ends, have a language in their hearts which is hard to understand. In Babel the language is confounded. This city is represented as a place of business, and those employed in it as merchants of the earth: "The merchants of the earth are waxed rich through the abundance of her delicacies" (Rev. 18 : 3).

And it is remarkable in this call that the language from the Father of Mercies is, "my people, come out of Babylon, my people." Thus his tender mercies are toward us in an imperfect state; and as we faithfully attend to the call, the path of righteousness is more and more opened; cravings which have not their foundation in pure wisdom more and more cease; and in an inward purity of heart we experience a restoration of that which was lost at Babel represented by the inspired prophet in the "returning of a pure language" (Zeph. 3:9).

Happy for them who humbly attend to the call, "Come out of Babylon, my people." For tho in going forth we may meet with trials which for a time may be painful, yet as we bow in true humility and continue in it, an evidence is felt that God only is wise; and that in weaning us from all that is selfish he prepares the way to a quiet habitation, where all our desires are bounded by his wisdom. And an exercise of spirit attends me, that we who are convinced of the pure leadings of truth may bow in the deepest reverence, and so watchfully regard this leader that many who are grievously entangled in a wilderness of vain customs may look upon us and be instructed. And O that such who have plenty of this world's goods may be faithful in that with which they are entrusted! and example others in the true Christian walking.

Our Blessed Savior, speaking on worldly greatness, compares himself to one waiting and attending on a company at dinner; "Whether is greater, he that sitteth at meat or he that serveth? Is not he that sitteth at meat? But I am amongst you as he that serveth" (Luke 22:27).

Thus in a world greatly disordered, where

men aspiring to outward greatness were wont
to oppress others to support their designs, he
who was of the highest descent, being the Son
of God and greater than any among the greatest families of men, by his example and doctrines foreclosed his followers from claiming
any show of outward greatness, from any supposed superiority in themselves or derived
from their ancestors.

He who was greater than earthly princes
was not only meek and low at heart, but his
outward appearance was plain and lowly, and
free from every stain of the spirit of this
world.

Such was the example of our blessed redeemer, of whom the beloved disciple said,
"He that saith he abideth in him, ought also
to walk even as he walked."

John Bradford, who suffered martyrdom under Queen Mary, wrote a letter to his friends
out of prison a short time before he was burned,
in which are these expressions; "Consider
your dignity as children of God, and temples
of the Holy Ghost, and members of Christ, be
ashamed therefore to think, speak, or do any
thing unseemly for God's children and the
members of Christ" (Fox's "Acts and Monu-
ments").

II
On the Example of Christ

As my mind hath been brought into a brotherly feeling with the poor, as to the things of this life, who are under trials in regard to getting a living in a way answerable to the purity of truth; a labor of heart hath attended me, that their way may not be made difficult through the love of money in those who are tried with plentiful estates, but that they with tenderness of heart may sympathize with them.

It was the saying of our blessed redeemer, "Ye can not serve God and mammon." There is a deep feeling of the way of purity, a way in which the wisdom of the world hath no part, but is opened by the Spirit of Truth, and is called the way to holiness; a way in which the traveler is employed in watching unto prayer; and the outward gain we get in this journey is considered as a trust committed to us by him who formed and supports the world, and is the rightful director of the use and application of the product of it.

Now except the mind be preserved chaste, there is no safety for us; but in an estrangement from true resignation the spirit of the world casts up a way in which gain is many times principally attended to, and in which there is a selfish application of outward treasures.

How agreeable to the true harmony of society is that exhortation of the apostle: "Look not every man on his own things, but every man also on the things of others. Let this mind be in you which was also in Christ Jesus." A person in outward prosperity may have the power of obtaining riches, but the same mind being in him which is in Christ Jesus, he may feel a tenderness of heart toward those of low degree; and instead of setting himself above them, may look upon it as an unmerited favor that his way through life is more easy than the way of many others; may improve every opportunity of leading forth out of those customs which have entangled the family; employ his time in looking into the wants of the poor members, and hold forth such a perfect example of humiliation that the pure witness may be reached in many minds and the way opened for a harmonious walking together.

Jesus Christ, in promoting the happiness of others, was not deficient in looking for the helpless who lay in obscurity, nor did he save any thing to render himself honorable among men which might have been of more use to the weak members in his father's family; of whose compassion toward us I may now speak a little. He who was perfectly happy in himself, moved with infinite love, "took not upon him the nature of angels," but our imperfect natures, and therein wrestled with the temptations which attend us in this life; and being the Son of him who is greater than earthly princes, yet became a companion to poor, sincere-hearted men; and tho he gave the clearest evidence that divine power attended him, yet the most unfavorable constructions were framed by a self-righteous people; those miracles represented as the effect of a diabolical power, and endeavors used to render him hateful, as having his mission from the prince of darkness; nor did their envy cease till they took him like a criminal and brought him to trial. Tho some may affect to carry the appearance of being unmoved at the apprehension of distress, our dear redeemer, who was perfectly sincere, having the same human nature which we have and feeling, a little before he was apprehended, the weight of that work upon him for which he came into the world, was "sorrowful even unto death"; here the human nature struggled to be excused from a cup so bitter; but his prayers centered in resignation, "Not my Will but thine be done." In this conflict, so great was his agony that "sweat like drops of blood fell from him to the ground."

Behold now, as foretold by the prophet, he is in a judicial manner numbered with the transgressors! Behold him as some poor man of no reputation, standing before the high priest and elders and before Herod and Pilate, where witnesses appear against him, and he, mindful of the most gracious design of his coming, declineth to plead in his own defense, "but as a sheep that is dumb before the shearer," so under many accusations, revilings, and buffetings remained silent. And tho he signified to Peter that he had access to power sufficient to overthrow all their outward forces, yet retaining a resignation to suffer for the sins of mankind, he exerted not that power, but permitted them to go on in their malicious designs and pronounce him to be worthy of death, even him who was perfect in goodness; thus "in his humiliation his judgment was taken away," and he, like some vile criminal, "led as a lamb to the slaughter." Under these heavy trials (tho poor unstable Pilate was convinced of his innocence, yet) the people generally looked upon him as a deceiver, a blasphemer, and the approaching punishment as a just judgment upon him; "They esteemed him smitten of God and afflicted." So great had been the surprize of his disciples at his being taken by armed men that they forsook him and fled; thus they hid their faces from him, he was despised, and by their conduct it appeared as tho they esteemed him not.

But contrary to that opinion of his being smitten of God and afflicted, it was for our sakes that "he was put to grief; he was wounded for our transgressions; he was bruised for our iniquities"; and under the weight of them manifesting the deepest compassion for the instruments of his misery, labored as their Advocate, and in the deeps of affliction, with an unconquerable patience, cried out, "Father, forgive them, they know not what they do!"

Now this mind being in us which was in Christ Jesus, it removes from our hearts the desire of superiority, worldly honor, or greatness; a deep attention is felt to the Divine Counselor, and an ardent engagement to promote, as far as we may be enabled, the happiness of mankind universally. This state, where every motion from a selfish spirit yieldeth to pure love, I may with gratitude to the Father of Mercies acknowledge, is often opened before me as a pearl to dig after; attended with a living concern that among the many nations and families on the earth those who believe in the Messiah, that "he was manifested to destroy the works of the devil," and thus to "take away the sins of the world," may experience the will of our Heavenly Father,

"may be done on earth as it is in heaven."
Strong are the desires I often feel that this
holy profession may remain unpolluted, and
the believers in Christ may so abide in the pure
inward feeling of his spirit, that the wisdom
from above may shine forth in their living,
as a light by which others may be instrument-
ally helped on their way, in the true harmonious walking.

III

On Merchandizing

Where the treasures of pure love are opened, and we obediently follow him who is the
light of life, the mind becomes chaste; and
a care is felt that the unction from the Holy
One may be our leader in every undertaking.

In being crucified to the world, broken off
from that friendship which is enmity with
God and dead to the customs and fashions
which have not their foundation in the truth,
the way is prepared to lowliness in outward
living, and to a disentanglement from those
snares which attend the love of money; and
where the faithful friends of Christ are so sit-
uated that merchandize appears to be their
duty, they feel a restraint from proceeding
farther than he owns their proceeding; being
convinced that "we are not our own, but are
bought with a price, that none of us may live

to ourselves, but to him who died for us" (2 Cor. 5:15). Thus they are taught not only to keep to a moderate advance and uprightness in their dealings, but to consider the tendency of their proceeding, to do nothing which they know would operate against the cause of universal righteousness, and to keep continually in view the spreading of the peaceable kingdom of Christ among mankind.

The Prophet Isaiah spake of the gathered church in the similitude of a city, where many being employed were all preserved in purity; "They shall call them the holy people, the redeemed of the Lord, and thou shalt be called, Sought out, a city not forsaken" (Isa. 63:10). And the apostle, after mentioning the mystery of Christ's sufferings, exhorts, "Be ye holy in all manner of conversation" (1 Pet. 1:15). There is a conversation necessary in trade; and there is a conversation so foreign from the nature of Christ's kingdom that it is represented in the similitude of one man pushing another with a warlike weapon; "There is that speaketh like the piercings of a sword" (Prov. 12:18). Now in all our concerns it is necessary that the leading of the Spirit of Christ be humbly waited for and faithfully followed, as the only means of being preserved chaste as an holy people, who "in all things are circumspect" (Ex. 23:13), that nothing we do may carry the appearance of approbation of the works of wickedness, make the unrighteous more at ease in unrighteousness, or occasion the injuries committed against the opprest to be more lightly looked over.

Where morality is kept to and supported by the inhabitants of a country, there is a certain reproach attends those individuals among them who manifestly deviate therefrom. But where iniquity is committed openly, and the authors of it are not brought to justice nor put to shame, their hands grow strong. Thus the general corruption of the Jews shortly before their state was broken up by the Chaldeans is described by their boldness in impiety; for as their leaders were connected together in wickedness, they strengthened one another and grew confident; "Were they ashamed when they had committed abominations? Nay, they were not at all ashamed, neither could they blush" (Jer. 6:15). On which account the Lord thus expostulates with them, "What hath my beloved to do in my house, seeing she hath wrought lewdness with many, and the holy flesh is passed from thee; when thou doest evil, then thou rejoicest" (Jer. 11:15).

Now the faithful friends of Christ, who hunger and thirst after righteousness and inwardly breathe that his kingdom may come on earth as it is in heaven, he teacheth them to be quick of understanding in his fear, and to be very attentive to the means he may appoint for promoting pure righteousness in the earth; and as shame is due to those whose works manifestly operate against the gracious design of his sufferings for us, a care lives on their minds that no wrong customs however supported may bias their judgments, but that they may humbly abide under the cross and be preserved in a conduct which may not contribute to strengthen the hands of the wicked in their wickedness, or to remove shame from those to whom it is justly due. The coming of that day is precious, in which we experience the truth of this expression, "The Lord our righteousness" (Jer. 23: 6), and feel him to be "made unto us wisdom and sanctification."

The example of a righteous man is often looked at with attention. Where righteous men join in business, their company gives encouragement to others; and as one grain of incense deliberately offered to the prince of this world renders an offering to God in that state unacceptable, and from those esteemed leaders of the people may be injurious to the weak; it requires deep humility of heart to follow him, who alone gives sound wisdom and the spirit of true discerning; and O how necessary it is to consider the weight of a holy profession!

The conduct of some formerly gave occasion of complaint against them; "Thou hast defiled thy sanctuaries by the multitude of thine iniquities, by the iniquity of thy traffic" (Ezek. 28:18), and in several places it is charged against Israel that they had polluted the holy name.

The prophet Isaiah represents inward sanctification in the similitude of being purged from that which is fuel for fire, and particularly describes the outward fruits brought forth by those who dwell in this inward holiness; "They walk righteously, and speak uprightly." By walking he represents the journey through life as a righteous journey; and by "speaking uprightly" seems to point at that which Moses appears to have had in view, when he thus exprest himself: "Thou shalt not follow a multitude to do evil, nor speak in a cause to decline after many to wrest judgment" (Ex. 23:2).

He goes on to show their firmness in equity, representing them as persons superior to all the arts of getting money which have not righteousness for their foundation, "They despise the gain of oppressions." And he further shows how careful they are that no prospects of gain may induce them to become partial in judgment respecting an injury; "They shake their hands from holding bribes."

Again, where any interest is so connected with shedding blood that the cry of innocent blood goes also with it, he points out their care to keep innocent blood from crying against them, in the similitude of a man's stopping his ears to prevent a sound from entering his head; "They stop their ears from hearing blood." And where they know that wickedness is committed, he points out with care that they do not by an unguarded friendship with the authors of it appear like unconcerned lookers on, but as people so deeply affected with sorrow, that they can not endure to stand by and behold it; this he represents in the similitude of a man "shutting his eyes from seeing evil."

"Who amongst us shall dwell with devouring fire? Who amongst us shall dwell with everlasting burnings? He that walketh righteously and speaketh uprightly. He that despiseth the gain of oppressions, that shaketh his hands from holding of bribes, that stoppeth his ears from hearing of blood, and shutteth his eyes from seeing evil" (Isa. 33: 15).

He proceeds in the spirit of prophecy to show how the faithful, being supported under temptations, would be preserved from that defilement that there is in the love of money; that as they who in a reverent waiting on

God feel their strength renewed are said to mount upward; so here their preservation from the snare of unrighteous gain is represented in the likeness of a man borne up above all crafty artful means of getting the advantage of another; "They shall dwell on high"; and points out the stability and firmness of their condition; "His place of defense shall be the munition of rocks"; and that under all the outward appearances of loss in denying himself of gainful profits for righteousness sake, yet through the care of him who provides for the sparrows he should have a supply answerable to his infinite wisdom; "Bread shall be given him, his waters shall be sure." And as our Savior mentions the sight of God to be attainable by the pure in heart, so here the prophet pointed out, how in true sanctification the understanding is opened to behold the peaceable, harmonious nature of his kingdom; "Thine eyes shall see the king in his beauty." And that looking beyond all the afflictions which attend the righteous, to "a habitation eternal in the heavens," they with an eye divinely open "shall behold the land that is very far off."

"He shall dwell on high, his place of defense shall be the munition of rocks, bread shall be given him, his waters shall be sure. Thine eyes shall see the king in his beauty;

they shall behold the land that is very far off'' (Isa. 33:16).

I often remember, and to me the subject is awful, that the great Judge of all the earth doeth that which is right, and that he, ''before whom the nations are as the drop of a bucket, is no Respecter of persons.'' Happy for them who, like the inspired prophet, ''in the way of his judgments wait for him'' (Isa. 26:8).

When we feel him to sit as a refiner with fire, and know a resignedness wrought in us to that which he appoints for us, his blessing in a very low estate is found to be more precious than much outward treasure in those ways of life where the leadings of his spirit are not followed.

The prophet, in a sight of a divine work among many people, declared in the name of the Lord, ''I will gather all nations and tongues, and they shall come and see my glory'' (Isa. 66:18). And again, ''From the rising of the sun to the going down of the same, my name shall be great amongst the gentiles, and in every place incense shall be offered to my name, and a pure offering'' (Mal. 1:11).

Behold here how the prophets had an inward sense of the spreading of the kingdom of Christ; and how he was spoken of as one who should ''take the heathen for his inheritance, and the utmost parts of the earth for

43

his possession'' (Ps. 2:8). That "he was given
for a light to the Gentiles; and for salvation
to the ends of the earth" (Isa. 49:6).

When we meditate on this divine work as a
work of ages, a work that the prophets felt
long before Christ appeared visibly on earth,
and remember the bitter agonies he endured
when he "poured out his soul unto death,"
that the heathen nations, as well as others,
might come to the knowledge of the truth and
be saved.

When we contemplate on this marvelous
work, as that which "the angels desire to look
into" (1 Pet. 1:12), and behold people
among whom this light hath eminently broken forth, and who have received many favors
from the bountiful hand of our Heavenly
Father; not only indifferent with respect to
publishing the glad tidings among the Gentiles, as yet sitting in darkness and entangled
with many superstitions, but aspiring after
wealth and worldly honors, take hold of means
to obtain their ends, tending to stir up wrath
and indignation, and to beget an abhorrence in
them to the name of Christianity—When these
things are weightily attended to, how mournful is the subject!

It is worthy of remembrance that people in
different ages, deeply baptized into the nature
of that work for which Christ suffered, have

joyfully offered up their liberty and lives for the promoting of it in the earth.

Policarp, who was reputed a disciple of the Apostle John, having attained to great age, was at length sentenced to die for his religion; and being brought to the fire, prayed nearly as follows: "Thou God and Father of our Lord Jesus Christ, by whom I have received the knowledge of thee! O God of the angels and powers, and of every living creature, and of all sorts of just men which live in thy presence, I thank thee, that thou hast graciously vouchsafed this day and this hour to allot me a portion among the number of martyrs, among the people of Christ, unto the resurrection of everlasting life; among whom I shall be received in thy sight this day as a fruitful and acceptable sacrifice; wherefore for all this, I praise thee, I bless thee, I glorify thee through the everlasting High Priest, Jesus Christ, thy well-beloved Son; to whom, with thee and the Holy Ghost, be all glory, world without end, AMEN."

Bishop Latimer, when sentence of death by fire was pronounced against him on account of his firmness in the cause of religion, he said, "I thank God most heartily, that he hath prolonged my life to this end; that I may in this case glorify him by this kind of death."

William Dewsbury, who had suffered much

for his religion, in his last sickness, encouraging his friends to faithfulness, made mention, like good old Jacob, of the loving-kindness of God to him in the course of his life, and that through the power of divine love he, for Christ's sake, had joyfully entered prisons.

I mention these as a few examples out of many of the powerful operations of the Spirit of Christ, where people are fully devoted to it, and of the ardent longings in their minds for the spreading of his kingdom among mankind. Now to those in the present age who truly know Christ, and feel the nature of his peaceable government opened in their understandings, how loud is that call wherewith we are called to faithfulness; that in following this pure light of life we, "as workers together with him," may labor in that great work for which he was offered as a sacrifice on the cross; and that his peaceable doctrines may shine through us in their real harmony, at a time when the name of Christianity is become hateful to many of the heathen.

When Gehazi had obtained treasures which the prophet under divine direction had refused, and was returned from the business, the prophet, troubled at his conduct, queried if it was a time thus to prepare for a specious living. "Is it a time to receive money and garments, men servants and maid servants?

The leprosy therefore of Naaman shall cleave to thee, and to thy seed for ever'' (2 Kings 5: 26). And O that we may lay to heart the condition of the present time, and humbly follow his counsel who alone is able to prepare the way for a true harmonious walking among mankind.

IV

On Divine Admonitions

Such are the perfections of our Heavenly Father that, in all the dispensations of his providence, it is our duty ''in every thing to give thanks.'' Tho from the first settlements of this part of America he hath not extended his judgments to the degree of famine, yet worms at times have come forth beyond numbering, and laid waste fields of grain and grass where they have appeared; another kind in great multitudes, working out of sight in grass ground, have so eaten the roots that the surface, being loosened from the soil beneath, might be taken off in great sheets. These kind of devouring creatures appearing seldom and coming in such multitudes, their generation appears different from most other reptiles, and by the prophet were called ''God's army sent amongst the people'' (Joel 2: 25).

There have been tempests of hail, which have very much destroyed the grain where

they extended. Through long drought in
summer, grain in some places hath been less
than half the usual quantity;[1] and in the continuance thereof, I have beheld with attention, from week to week, how dryness from the
top of the earth hath extended deeper and
deeper, while the corn and plants have lan-
guished; and with reverence my mind hath
been turned toward him who, being perfect in
goodness, in wisdom and power, doeth all
things right. And after long drought, when
the sky hath grown dark with a collection of
matter, and clouds like lakes of water hung
over our heads, from whence the thirsty land
hath been soaked; I have at times with awful-
ness beheld the vehement operation of lightning, made sometimes to accompany these
blessings, as a messenger from him who created all things to remind us of our duty in a
right use of those benefits, and give striking
admonitions that we do not misapply those
gifts, in which an almighty power is exerted
in bestowing them upon us.

When I have considered that many of our
fellow creatures suffer much in some places
for want of the necessaries of life, while those
who rule over them are too much given to
luxury and divers vanities; and behold the

[1] When crops fail, I often feel a tender care that the
case of poor tenants may be mercifully considered.

apparent deviation from pure wisdom among us in the use of the outward gifts of God; those marks of famine have appeared like humbling admonitions from him, that we might be instructed by gentle chastisements, and might seriously consider our ways; remembering that the outward supply of life is a gift from our Heavenly Father, and no more venture to use or apply his gifts in a way contrary to pure wisdom.

Should we continue to reject those merciful admonitions, and use his gifts at home contrary to the gracious design of the giver, or send them abroad in a way of trade which the Spirit of Truth doth not lead into; and should he whose eyes are upon all our ways extend his chastisements so far as to reduce us to much greater distress than hath yet been felt by these provinces; with what sorrow of heart might we meditate on that subject: "Hast thou not procured this unto thyself, in that thou hast forsaken the Lord thy God, when he led me by the way? Thine own wickedness shall correct thee, and thy backslidings shall reprove thee; know therefore, and see that it is an evil thing and bitter, that thou hast forsaken the Lord thy God, and that my fear is not in thee, saith the Lord of Hosts" (Jer. 2:17,19).

My mind hath often been affected with sorrow in beholding a wrong application of the

gifts of our Heavenly Father; and those expressions concerning the defilement of the
earth have been opened to my understanding;
"The earth was corrupt before God, and the
earth was filled with violence" (Gen. 6:11).
Again (Isa. 24:5). "The earth also is defiled under the inhabitants thereof."

The earth being the work of a divine power,
may not as such be accounted unclean; but
when violence is committed thereon, and the
channel of righteousness so obstructed that
"in our skirts are found the blood of the souls
of poor innocents; not by a secret search, but
upon all these" (Jer. 2:34).

When blood shed unrighteously remains un-
atoned for, and the inhabitants are not effectually purged from it, when they do not
wash their hands in innocency, as was figured
in the law, in the case of one being found slain;
but seek for gain arising from scenes of violence and oppression, here the land is polluted
with blood (Deut. 21:6).

Moreover, when the earth is planted and
tilled, and the fruits brought forth are applied
to support unrighteous purposes; here the
gracious design of Infinite Goodness, in these
his gifts being perverted, the earth is defiled;
and the complaint formerly uttered becomes
applicable; "Thou hast made me to serve with
thy sins; thou hast wearied me with thine
iniquities" (Isa. 43:24).

SELECTIONS FROM
Addresses to the Deity

BY

JAMES FORDYCE, D.D.

JAMES FORDYCE

Scotch divine and author, was born at Aberdeen 1720; died at Bath October 1, 1796. He was educated at the high school in Aberdeen and at Marischal College. On February 23, 1743, he was licensed by the Aberdeen presbytery, and ordained at Brechin on August 28, 1743. From there he went to Alloa, Clackmannanshire, October 12, 1753, and in 1760 became successor to Dr. Samuel Lawrence, minister of the Monkwell Street Presbyterian congregation, London. In 1782 he resigned this office. Among his published works are the following: "The Eloquence of the Pulpit" (1752); "The Temple of Virtue" (1757); "The Folly...of Unlawful Pleasures" (1760); "Sermons to Young Women" (1765); "The Character and Conduct of the Female Sex" (1776); "Addresses to Young Men" (1777); "Addresses to the Deity" (1785); "Poems" (1786); "A Discourse on Pain" (1791).

A View of the Sea

["The first address turns on a View of the Sea from a temple at High Cliff, near Christ-Church, Hampshire. The second has for its subject, Salvation by Christ, and was intended as a sequel to the former. The third, on Contemplation, grew out of both."—From the Preface.]

1. From this temple, seated on a lofty cliff, and open on every side, to behold the beauty and grandeur of thy works, Almighty Maker, from this terrestrial temple, permit an humble, but delighted worshiper, to lift his heart and voice toward thy glorious sanctuary in heaven. Vouchsafe to receive his address, proceeding from no hypocritical lips, but from a deep and reverential conviction of thy august presence, thou all-pervading Deity. Pardon whatever thy pure eyes discern amiss in thy frail, offending creature, whose only trust is in thy infinite mercy; and raise his thoughts to the elevation of his theme.

2. In this place of security, I view unaffrighted, tho not unawed, the majestic ocean spread out before me. Stupendous image of thy power, Omnipotent Creator; nor yet less of thy benevolence, universal Parent! Was it not formed by thee, to unite in bonds of mutual intercourse thy wide-extended family of mankind, to carry through various and distant nations the respective productions and

discoveries of each, to relieve or diminish their mutual wants, and disseminate the blessings of knowledge and humanity unto the ends of the earth?

3. I lament before thee, Heavenly Father, that this illustrious instance of thy goodness hath, by the depravity of men, been often perverted to far other purposes. How often, alas, is it made subservient to the worst designs of avarice and ambition, to wicked policy, hostile invasion and desolating war! Praised be that divine revelation, which opens a prospect into better days. "Let the floods clap their hands, the multitude of the isles shout for joy, and the inhabitants of the world break forth into singing." The great Messiah's kingdom will come, in all its plenitude of happiness. Sin and sorrow will flee away; injustice and oppression give place to righteous laws and good government; and freedom, truth, and peace be established on foundations firm as yonder rocks, broad as that sea, and permanent as the everlasting hills.

4. When from this height I look abroad upon the boundless deep as far as my eye can reach; when raising it "I consider thy heavens, the work of thy fingers"; when at night, assisted by the telescope, I more accurately contemplate "the moon and the stars which thou hast ordained"; when from a survey so vast

and astonishing I strive to frame the most
enlarged conceptions of thy creation, and of
thyself, I am lost in the immensity which sur-
rounds me; I am overwhelmed by that infini-
tude which I can never comprehend; I am
utterly confounded at my own littleness,
amidst the spacious universe, and from the
depth of self-abasement can only breathe out
the language of thy ancient servant, "What
is man that thou art mindful of him, or the
son of man that thou visitest him?" In himself, O Lord, he is nothing, yea, "less than
nothing, and vanity." But by thy favorable
regard, whose condescension is equal to thy
greatness, he rises to importance and dignity.
"For thou hast made him a little lower than
the angels, and hast crowned him with glory
and honor. Thou madest him to have
dominion over the works of thy hands: thou
hast put all things under his feet; all sheep and
oxen; yea, and the beasts of the field, the fowl
of the air, and the fish of the sea, and whatsoever passeth through the paths of the sea."

5. But who can number the tribes, or tell
the diversity of living creatures, with which
thou hast replenished this mighty receptacle
of waters; fitting all to enjoy their native element, and many to supply a rich and whole-
some nourishment for man? May he receive
it with thanksgiving, as one of those benefits,

that, when placed within his power, were intended to employ his industry, and strengthen him for thy service! Nor would I forget to acknowledge that benignant providence, which hast in so many other ways rendered the same element conducive to health and comfort, by furnishing stores of salt to season and preserve our food, by refreshing the adjacent coasts with salutary breezes, by invigorating the weak and restoring the diseased that bathe in its briny waves.

6. Neither doth thy kindness, Father of Mercies, stop here. To all the rest thou hast superadded entertainment for the contemplative mind, in that marvelous variety of things, both small and great, with which thou hast adorned the shores, the rocks, and the caverns of the sea; which, the more they are sought out by such as take pleasure in them, must ever be admired the more. And how conspicuous, O God, are thy power, thy wisdom, and thy watchful care, in binding with a girdle of sand the impetuous main, so that its mightiest billows can not break through to overflow the earth and drown the nations, as at the general deluge; while the winds and tides, in ever-changing succession, purify its waters, present a prospect always new, and further by thy blessing the beneficial communications of trade and commerce! "Oh that men would praise

the Lord for his goodness, and for his wonderful works to the children of men!"

7. Now the sky is serene: the sun shines forth in his strength: the sea is smoothed into a liquid plain; and gentle gales, sporting on its surface, waft alike the stately vessel and the little bark. Preserver of mankind, guard them in their course, and bring them to their desired haven. When arrived there, let them not forget to whom they owe their safety. And may all "who go down to the sea in ships, and see thy wonders in the deep," learn to seek thy protection, and fortify their hearts against the dangers that encompass them, not by blind courage, or brutal insensibility, but by "doing justly, loving mercy, and walking humbly with thee!"

8. Let the wicked tremble at the terrors of the ocean, lest it swallow them up in its fury, and they sink into a yet more tremendous abyss, prepared by thy justice for the workers of iniquity. But from threatening rocks and lurking quicksands, from the howling tempest, the yawning gulph, and the thick darkness, dreadful to conscious guilt, what have the righteous ultimately to fear? Art not thou their Father and their Friend? Art not thou "the God of the sea, as well as of the dry land?" Are not they still within the embrace of thy supporting arm? Thou wilt be their

refuge in the time of trouble. Thou wilt save them from impending shipwreck, or deliver them from the midst of its horrors, and guide their enfeebled but grateful steps to the dwellings of pity, where they shall find shelter and consolation; or else, if it be thy pleasure to set them for ever beyond the reach of calamity and peril, thou wilt receive their spirits into thy paternal bosom.

9. Roll on, ye destined ages, till the plans of providence are all fulfilled. At length the morning of the resurrection will dawn, when the sea shall give up its prey, and the dead shall rise incorruptible. Happy period! Consummation most devoutly to be wished! Then shall I meet in perfect glory a much-loved and long-lamented brother; the stay of his father's house, the comfort of his widowed mother, my counselor and example in youth; of whom the devouring waves were permitted to bereave us, at the instant that we were rejoicing in hope to welcome his return from foreign lands, full of honor, and rich in accumulated treasures of learning, eloquence, and wisdom. So it seemed good in thy sight, mysterious, unerring Ruler. "Clouds and darkness are round about thee; but righteousness and judgment are the habitation of thy throne." That inestimable man was taken from the evil to come. By an end, which

ignorance or impatience would have deemed untimely, of what public disasters and private sorrows did he not escape the pain of partaking! With what congratulations would his venerable ancestors and a bright circle of seraphic spirits hail his enlightened and benevolent soul, on gaining so early the shore of immortality! With what transports, till then unfelt, would his rising faculties join that high assembly, to celebrate the praise of his and their Parent and Lord!

10. Nor wilt thou be angry, if emulating such celestial harmony, I presume to add my imperfect note. Art thou not also my Parent and my Lord, altho I am yet "a sojourner on earth?" Deign to receive my humble tribute of love and homage. Accept my warmest gratitude, in particular, for having formed me capable of these contemplations, and inclined my heart to entertain them. Let me never think of thy majesty but with the deepest veneration; never dare to mention thy name with rashness or indifference; nor live to become a careless spectator of the beautiful and magnificent objects, in which thou hast manifested thy perfections with such surpassing glory. May the spirit of devotion they have at this time called forth be nourished and increased by frequent reflections on a scene so peculiarly adapted, as that which I

behold, to exalt the imagination and strike the mind with inexpressible solemnity. May I ever study to keep my passions in subjection to the awful Power "who saith to the sea, hither shalt thou come, but no farther: here shall thy proud waves be staid." And let that irresistible voice which stills their rage command every tumult of my breast into a calm.

11. When from the immediate effects of thy omnipotence, great Creator, I turn to observe the inferior works of men, I would not forget that divine energy, without which nothing noble, useful, or pleasing can be accomplished. To this secret but powerful influence I trace the proportions, accommodations, and ornaments of the goodly fabric which now attracts my attention. The skill that contrived, and the diligence that executed the whole, were from thee, O God, the Giver of every talent, and the Inspirer of every virtue. To thee its master looks up with reverence. Thy workmanship in nature thou hast disposed him to study through all its visible degrees, from whatever is most extensive and sublime, to its most minute and seemingly inconsiderable parts; inconsiderable, only to superficial beholders. To his, and to every eye illuminated by science, and strengthened by the microscopic glass, the smallest are not less distinguished than the greatest by the signatures

of supreme intelligence. From the delight and improvement attending such occupations, incline him daily to aspire after a higher existence, in which he may "see thee face to face," and contemplate with unceasing admiration the issues of almighty wisdom and goodness in their source. While he remains in this state of imperfection, may he ever seek his happiness in the pursuit of truth, in the practise of temperance, in the works of charity, in the pleasures of a philosopher, and of a Christian! And from these may he ever derive that sincere satisfaction which neither opulence, nor rank, nor power could bestow!

12. For myself, thy unworthy servant, I will bless thee while I live, that in the decline of my days thou art giving me to enjoy the leisure and serenity of a peaceful retreat, where by pious meditation and fervent prayer, a ready submission to thy providence, and a growing complacency in thy works, the constant exercise of good will toward men, and the elevating hope of the gospel, I may double my diligence to prepare for the inevitable hour. And when it shall arrive, grant, most merciful Father, through the mediation of my divine Master and only Savior, that I may obtain an easy passage from this to a happier region, and be admitted to worship thee in the temples of eternity. AMEN.

On Salvation By Christ

1. Supreme of Beings, I have seen thy glory
in thy works; more especially in the world of
waters created by thy hand, controlled by thy
authority, and by thy gracious providence
directed to ends the most important and beneficial. I have also, in the efforts of human art,
seen that omnipotent agency which operates
through all, without which there is nothing
wise and nothing strong. Separate from thee,
"man in his best estate is altogether vanity,"
the child of weakness, and the heir of sorrow.
United to thy sovereign spirit, he is solaced,
magnanimous, and blessed; unappalled by
danger, and unconquered by distress. "Un-
derneath him are everlasting arms." He shall
pass in security "through the fire, and through
the water." "The water shall not overflow
him, nor the fire kindle upon him." Strengthened by thy power, and animated by a sense
of thy favor, he shall triumph over death itself, tho assailing him in its most terrible
array. The fiercest conflagration, or the
blackest tempest, would only convey him
sooner to the bosom of untroubled rest in the
regions of immortal day. "The ungodly are
not so, but are like the chaff which the wind
driveth away." This wide creation affords

not safety to thy enemies. "If they take the
wings of the morning, and fly to the utmost
part of the sea, even there shall thy hand find
them, and thy right hand" press them into
misery. But who can tell what aggravated
woes await the impenitent beyond the
boundary of time? Who can unfold the horrors of outer darkness? Ah, may I never
know what it is to fall without hope under
the weight of thy displeasure, great Almighty!

2. But how shall I escape it? "I have
sinned against heaven, and in thy sight," my
Father, my Benefactor, and my God, whom
by numberless ties of duty, gratitude, justice,
piety, I was bound to serve and honor. I am
overwhelmed with confusion at the sight of
my unworthiness in so pure a presence. This
beautiful temple, this noble eminence, the
majestic ocean, now assuming its mildest form,
and with redoubled luster giving back the
rays of the sun, those exhilarating scenes, that
so lately inspired me with gladness, are on a
sudden become ineffectual to cheer. To me
nature smiles in vain, when I think of having
offended the Lord of nature. Where shall I
look, or whither shall I turn, for relief under
the painful recollection.

3. Propitious Divinity, I behold an object[1]
that instantly consoles me, by calling to my

---

[1] Christ-Church in the neighborhood.

remembrance thy willingness to pardon and to save. My heart leaps for joy at the name of thine anointed, the meek and lowly King of Zion, the loving and beloved deliverer of mankind. Loudly would I celebrate thy perfections as displayed in this wondrous frame of things. But in the more wondrous works of redemption they shine with superior splendor, and demand a nobler song.

4. In creation I contemplate a world produced from unresisting chaos. In redemption, I see it recovered from the darkness and disorder of wilful transgression. "In the beginning thy Spirit moved upon the face of the deep," and a fair harmonious universe arose. "Thou spakest the word, and it was done: thou gavest the command, and it stood fast." But how often didst thou speak to sinners, and they regarded thee not! They heard unconcerned the thunder of heaven; nor did the melody of earth allure them to their duty. While the creatures above and below addrest them on thy behalf, they refused to harken; till, touched and won by thy tender mercies in Christ Jesus, they yielded to the charm of divine love, and fled from their sins to a forgiving Deity.

5. Long had they defied the threatenings of thy law, and despised the warnings of the prophets. Miracles of power astonished, but

did not reform them. Miracles of deliverance were followed only with a passing impression. Frequent chastisement was soon forgotten; and infinite forbearance but hardened them the more. At last, when the fulness of time was come, Christ appeared, the Image of thy benevolence, the Minister of thy grace; and a word, a look, from him sufficed to melt the heart with contrition, and bend the will into obedience.

6. It was not by worldly might, or royal magnificence, by the arts of policy, or the pomp of eloquence; it was not by promising aught that is of highest estimation among the sons of earth, nor yet by sparing their corruptions or countenancing their errors; it was not by any or by all of these, that the Son of thy love obtained his victories over the minds of men. Triumphs among the foolish, the sensual, and the proud; triumphs gained by means that served only to soothe them in their blindness, to nourish their crimes, and augment their misery; the vain and superficial triumphs of a day he left to those that admired and pursued them. His was a far different design; "to turn men from darkness unto light, and from the power of Satan" to the practise of righteousness and the glories of immortality. In prosecution of his benevolent purpose, he graciously stooped to assume

our nature, "and make himself of no reputation." But, as tho it were not sufficient to
veil his original honors with the garment of
frail humanity, he submitted "to take upon
him the form of a servant," to be born in the
lowest condition, and the meanest circumstances; to become "a man of sorrows and
acquainted with grief, despised and rejected
of men, and not to have where to lay his head."
Thus it pleased him, who could have com-
manded the riches and applause of the world,
to throw a shade upon both, that neither might
be esteemed by his followers necessary to happiness. And at length, to impress them more
deeply with the greatness of humility, the
worth of resignation, and the transcendent
excellence of divine charity, he voluntarily
suffered a painful and ignominious death for
their sins.

7. Blessed be he that came in the name of
the Lord, to save us, that came in thy name,
Almighty Father, invested with pre-eminent
authority, "anointed with the oil of gladness
above his fellows." To prove his commission
from thee, he performed works which no man
had ever performed; "he spake as no man
ever spake. Grace was poured into his lips."
He convinced and penetrated his hearers by
the simplicity of truth: he astonished and
awed them by its majesty. The clouds and

darkness that rested on a future existence he removed, as far as was expedient for those who were ordained to "live by faith, and not by sight." The retributions of eternity he set before them in language the most powerful and affecting. Pointing to the narrow but pleasant path of heaven, he earnestly called them to follow him thither. "The broad" but treacherous "way, that leadeth to destruction," he no less kindly admonished them to shun. The upright however obscure, the penitent however censured by men, he received and encouraged with ineffable mildness and condescension. He comforted them that mourned. "He fed his flock like a shepherd: he gathered the lambs with his arm, carried them in his bosom, and gently led those that were with young." His life exhibited a pattern of lowliness and goodness, of patient affliction and heroic self-denial before unseen; and his death upon the cross was a sacrifice worthy of thy acceptance. There he manifested the perfection of obedience; there "he suffered, the just for the unjust, that he might bring us to thee." By his humiliation "they who humble themselves, shall be exalted"; by his atonement they who obey him are saved. But, blessed God, who can speak the power of his resurrection, the grandeur of his ascension, the prevalence of his mediation, or the triumphs of his everlasting gospel? Who can represent the beauty or efficacy of this last and best dispensation? "It is the doing of the Lord, and marvellous in our eyes." Nor in ours only. Well may you, ye spirits of light, pry with eagerness and wonder into this great mystery. Well might you, ye sons of God, ye holy and benevolent angels, sing together, and shout for joy, at the restoration of a fallen universe. "Glory to God in the highest: on earth peace: good will toward men!"

8. Merciful heaven, what prospects rise to my enraptured view! All old things are done away: "behold, all things are become new." The light of truth dawns upon the darkest minds, like that of the morning on the benighted traveler. The lowest disciple of thy Son is wiser than the greatest teachers of pagan philosophy. The sweetness of pardon descends into the hearts of the contrite, "like rain upon the mowen grass." The humble and sincere are called to rejoice in the assurance of salvation. The souls of men are renovated by thy spirit, as the face of the earth is revived by returning spring. The agitations of appetite and the storms of passion subside into a sacred calm. Discord and hatred, malice, envy, and mad ambition, vanish before the "Prince of Peace." Crowns and scepters

are laid at his feet. All the charities walk in
his train. Virtue is invigorated by faith, and
gathers from the cross wreaths of immortality.
I am transported with the thought, that, as
Christ was "delivered for our offenses, so he
rose again for our justification. He is the
resurrection and the life: whosoever believe
in him, though they were dead, they shall yet
live." Our bodies, now the seat of so many
disorders, the source of so many snares, the
occasion of so much toil and care, at last the
prey of corruption, shall one day assume a
higher and happier form. They shall spring
from the dishonors of the grave, at the voice
of the archangel, by the power of Jesus; and
"we shall be like him, because we shall see
him as he is." We shall dwell for ever in his
animating presence; forever free from pain;
subject to sickness, decay, and dissolution no
more; arrayed in perfect beauty, secured in
perfect innocence; and, by his approving sentence, exalted to felicity unutterable and endless. With such prospects and such hopes,
what have thy servants to fear, or why should
our hearts be troubled, in life or in death?

9. But ah, my God, how shall those "escape,
who neglect so great salvation?" Open, I
beseech thee, their eyes, to see their dangerous
estate, the necessity of immediate amendment,
the insufficiency of human aid. Inspire them

with faith in the sovereign physician, who
alone can cure the maladies of the soul; till restored to spiritual health, and filled with joy
and thankfulness, they are enabled "to run in
the way of thy commandments." May such as
are ready to sink under the burden of conscious guilt and disorder, fighting in secret for
deliverance, and longing after the pure and
peaceful pleasures of religion, perceive themselves supported by the grace of Jesus! Dispose them to accept the invitation of that
divine philanthropist who said, "Come unto
me, all ye that labor and are heavy laden,
and I will give you rest." May they have the
happiness to feel that he is "mighty to save!"
May they firmly believe, that he is too just to
"break the bruised reed," too generous to
take advantage of lamented folly or involun-
tary weakness, too faithful not to fulfil the
word on which he hath caused his servants in
all generations to rely.

10. For such as, after manifold engage-
ments and solemn vows, have forsaken his
service, "denying the Lord that bought them,
and opening the mouths of his enemies to
blaspheme," "Father of Mercies, hear my
prayer, and renew them again by repentance."
May they instantly flee the occasions that en-
snared them, and, like Peter, weep bitterly;
nor ever cease to cherish a tender and in-

genuous sorrow, till by unwearied supplications, the strictest vigilance, and the severest self-denial they are recovered to their duty and to thy favor. Permit me also, O my God, to intercede for those unhappy men that have to this day rejected equally the claims and the offers of him who came to redeem them. Awaken their attention; conquer their prejudices; teach them, before it be too late, to consider well the danger of opposing his authority whom thou hast "set as King upon thy holy hill of Zion." To whom, for his obedience unto death, thou hast "given a name above every name, that at the name of Jesus every knee might bow, and every tongue confess"; of whom Moses spake; whom the prophets long before his appearing foretold, and to whom the apostles, that had seen him after his resurrection, gave witness; who while he abode on earth wrought miracles of unexampled power and beneficence, and when he ascended into heaven, qualified his ministers to preach and propagate his religion among the nations. And where, O Lord, have its adversaries found an institution alike honorable to thy perfections, alike suited to the wants and wishes of mankind, fraught with equal consolation to the penitent and the afflicted, formed alike to render its disciples virtuous and humble, peaceable and gentle, moderate in prosperity, patient in suffering, "stedfast and immovable, and always abounding in good works?" If they have not found, if they can not find aught to be compared with this glorious light, would they quench it in their rage, and leave in its place shadows and phantoms, unavailing conjectures, distracting doubts, and endless uncertainty? Blessed God, what will they do, "when their feet shall stumble on the dark mountains?" Who shall comfort them in their last agonies? Who shall plead for them at the judgment-seat of him whose power they disputed or defied, whose proffered friendship they treated with scorn?

11. And where, alas! shall those appear who call him "Lord, Lord, but do not the things which he saith"; false pretenders to zeal and sanctity; proud and uncharitable "hypocrites, who trust in themselves that they are righteous, and despise others; enemies to the cross of Christ," who would transform it into an instrument of unrighteousness, which it was designed to destroy; who would make him "the minister of sin, that died to redeem them from all iniquity?" Searcher of hearts, discover them to themselves, in their aggravated guilt and wretchedness. Convince them, that their pretenses are vain, and their professions impious; that "without works faith is dead," and without sincerity, religion but

a name which can not impose on thy omniscience, and will only draw upon them heavier condemnation. Spare them, O God, to repent of their great wickedness, endue them with integrity, and teach them to "worship thee, who art a Spirit, in spirit and in truth."

12. Preserve me, most merciful Father, from hypocrisy, self-deceit, and all uncharitableness. Preserve me from doubting, for a moment, the divine evidence of the gospel, or distrusting, even in the darkest hour, the wisdom and benignity of its Author. Oh, preserve me from the baseness of denying him on any occasion. And "God forbid that I should glory, save in his cross." By the power of his cross may I be crucified to the love of the world, with all its short unsatisfying vanities! And finally grant, that being reconciled to thee by his death and intercession, instructed in thy will by his doctrine and precepts, and by his example, promises, and aid conformed to it, I may look up to thy throne with hope of acceptance, behold the purity of thy nature tempered with paternal grace, revere and love thee at the same time, admire and rejoice in thy works more and more, and from all I see above, around, and below, rise with increasing ardors of devotion to the Fountain of goodness and of happiness. AMEN.

On Contemplation

1. Delighted with the blessings and wonders of creation, transported by the yet higher wonders and blessings of redemption, my soul would ascend with fresh aspirations to thee, O God, the origin of both; to thee, the greatest and best of beings, the greatest because the best; from whom alone proceeds whatever is good and great; to whom, therefore, be all the glory from all thy reasonable offspring. To praise thee, thou sovereign Parent, is surely the most becoming exercise of reason; and they are the happiest who perform it most worthily—the bright assembly of saints and seraphim, who circle thy throne rejoicing and with unbroken harmony celebrate thy perfections. Fain would thy servant here below anticipate their joys. Fain would he learn their language, and join, however feebly, their elevated chorus, "the Lord God omnipotent reigneth, hallelujah!"

2. Compassionate Father, forgive the languor and unevenness with which my spirit, prest down by the weight of mortality, attempts so high a service. Ah, that my heart were in better tune, and more alive to gratitude,

love, and admiration, to the noblest affections of every mind in unison with the melody
of nature, and of heaven! Almighty Maker,
assist my weak endeavors. Let no jarring
passion disturb my thoughts. Teach me to
correct every irregular movement, and diligently to cherish that spirit of pious contemplation which soothes the breast into serenity, supplies devotion with its amplest strains,
and lifts the faculties to him who gave them.

3. What shall I render, O Lord, for the
exalted satisfaction of tracing thy attributes
in this capacious universe, for the transcendent privilege of walking with thee, amidst
the glory of thy works? Dispose me more at-
tentively to study, tho I can never fully comprehend, them. Unable as I am in a survey
so immense and so various, to discover the
contrivance or the use of many parts, I have
yet abundant cause to believe that they are
worthy of their Author; such consistency of
design, such consummate wisdom, such
boundless goodness are conspicuous in all
the rest! I rejoice in the reflection that the
farther inquiry is extended by the largest
and most enlightened minds, they meet yet
brighter marks of intelligence and benignity and are more fully convinced that those
appearances which the ignorant and the dis-
contented have censured as blemishes in the

plan, or defects in the execution, are to be numbered among the strongest demonstrations of thy skill and care, Almighty Architect. But, O my God, if views which this limited state of humanity renders at the utmost imperfect yield so much delight, what will it be when every remaining cloud that now obscures thy workmanship shall vanish, and the light of eternity, breaking forth on our transported eyes, shall give us to behold it in all its magnitude and splendor?

4. The whole creation is full of thee. Forbid that the beauty, or diversity which it displays, should become a veil to hide thee from my sight, where, "by the things that are made, thy power and Godhead may be clearly seen." Where, for the trial of my faith, thou art pleased "to hold back the face of thy throne," may I still perceive the influence of the present divinity, and still adore the great supreme! When from that elevated throne I am favored with the radiations of light and mercy, may I lay myself open to them with thankfulness, humility and meekness!

5. "Where is the wise? where is the scribe? where is the disputer of this world?" Thou hast shown me, O Lord, that "professing to be wise, they become fools." Their confidence abuses their understanding. Beguiled

by the glare of novelty, and fired by the ambition of fame for freedom of thought and discernment above others, in matters where docility and diffidence are chiefly required, they turn from the sober pursuit of truth, and are led away into pernicious errors. "The heavens declare thy glory; and the firmament showeth thy handiwork. Day unto day uttereth speech; and night unto night teacheth knowledge." The eloquence of the creation, proclaiming thy greatness, and pleading for thy rights, is heard and understood by the honest but unpretending believer, by the self-denied and single-hearted worshiper. Neither the illiterate hind nor the untutored savage have been wholly insensible to the language of nature. But the ungodly man, who is spoiled by vain philosophy and perplexed "by the oppositions of science falsely so called, stoppeth his ear, like the deaf adder, and will not hear the voice of the charmer, though charming never so wisely." Misled by the cavils of infidelity, and lost in the maze of metaphysics, he wanders forever in a dark and crooked path, farther and yet farther from the straight and cheerful road that leads to everlasting day.

6. Save me, Heavenly Father, from the boasted benevolence of those who, while they promise liberty from the shackles of super-

stition and prejudice, are laboring to overthrow every principle which thou hast established among mankind as the foundation of their virtue and their happiness. Deliver me from the false pretexts of those whose "tender mercies are cruelty"; who would rob the fainting spirit of its richest cordial, tear from the children of sorrow their most powerful support, and leave without reward or expectation the generous toils of the true patriot, the useful and arduous researches of the devout philosopher, the patient conflicts and heroic sacrifices of the follower of Jesus. May I ever regard with abhorrence their impious system, who would transform this beautiful and glorious universe into a scene of desolation, excluding thy creative energy, and banishing that sovereign presence which directs, enlivens, and adorns it! Defend, I beseech thee, every virtuous mind and every unwary youth from the deceitfulness of all that are wickedly striving to undermine and destroy "whatsoever things are just, and true, and venerable," and holy among men, whatsoever things can endear them to each other as members of thy family or recommend them to thee as subjects of thy government, whatsoever things become their dignity and their hopes as immortal beings. Inspire them with an utter and unabating detestation

of that depravity which, not contented to disturb the peace and order of human life, seeks
with frigid argumentation, deliberate subtle-
ty, or wanton mirth, to damp and degrade
the heaven-born soul that was made after
thine image, and at last to sink it with all
its faculties and honors into the fearful
abyss of nothing.

7. But, blessed Creator, is it indeed possible that such indignity to thee, such insensibility to the dearest interests of human
kind, should be found in creatures called ra-
tional? Alas! who can tell to what strong
delusions those may be abandoned in thy
righteous judgment, who so profanely per-
vert the invaluable gift of reason, who turn
it so audaciously against the Giver? Most
truly hath thy word declared that "the fool
hath said in his heart, there is no God." In
his heart the malady begins. "Through the
pride of his heart, he will not seek after thee."
Thy justice is offended, and he is conscious
of his danger. He secretly hates the power
whom he dreads. His evil passions, whether
more open or disguised, increase his aversion
to thy laws. Thence he is eager to question
thy existence. He wishes and strives to dis-
believe it. He wishes and strives in vain.
However he may argue, whatever he may
boast, chilling apprehensions will arise:

specters of horror will haunt him in the silent watches of the night; they will pursue him at noon-day; in the midst of society they will poison his pleasures, nor will the voice of laughter or the face of gaiety prove him to be free from inward anguish. His conscience takes part with thee. "Thy terrors make him afraid": thy thunder startles, thy lightning flashes conviction into his soul. Altho in his folly he "makes a mock of sin, and utters great swelling words of vanity"; when pain, and grief, and sickness, and decay come upon him, where shall he find refuge from thy displeasure? Whither shall he flee from himself? One resource, one dreadful resource, he hath long endeavored to hope may yet remain; that when the last messenger arrives, he shall escape in a night eternal.

8. Merciful Deity, is there then no other resource for this man, no better refuge? Permit thy sinful servant, who hath "tasted and seen that thou art good," to implore thy pity for a fellow creature that little thought, when he entered on "the error of his way," how far it might entice him from truth and happiness! Spare him, O Lord, spare him to repent, if it be not yet too late. Change his heart by thy almighty Spirit, if consistent with the laws of thy righteous government. Would there not be "joy among the angels

that are in heaven," if by an extraordinary contrition and a triumphant faith this very man were made a trophy of peculiar grace?

9. But however thy unerring will may determine in respect to him and offenders of his enormity, hear me, Parent of benevolence, oh! hear me, when with redoubled fervor I beseech thee to guard the young and the ingenuous from the snares of unbelief. Lead them forth into the lovely and instructive walks of nature. Dispose them to view, with the serious collected eye of contemplation, the spacious earth, the boundless sea, the awful rocks, the lofty hills, and the fruitful valleys; the fields, the flocks, and the herds; the springs and the rivers, with "the green pastures by the still waters"; the solemn woods and groves; the cheerful garden adorned with trees, and herbs, and flowers, "after their kind"; the smiling sky, and yonder refulgent sun. In these may they learn to admire thy perfections! And when from these they look upon themselves, and see how "wonderfully they are made," and feel that multiplied delights thou hast given them to know, may they reflect with gladness that they live, not in a forlorn and fatherless world, but in a creation over which the Creator presides; may they acknowledge with gratitude and devotion that

"thou art in all, and through all, and over all, God blessed for ever," and ever inclined to bless thy children.

10. Heavenly Father, what satisfaction is his who, often withdrawing from the tumult of business and the noise of folly, flies to the sanctuary of divine meditation, there recovers the composure of his mind, enjoys undisturbed tranquility, and tastes that peace of thine "which passeth all understanding!" What improvement, when in the silence of the passions he harkens with profound attention to thy voice within him, prompting each pious thought, each charitable deed, each ardent desire after immortality! What elevation, when conversant with the order and beneficence displayed on every side, he is taught to admire, and admiring to copy them, till he becomes like thee, "holy as thou art holy, and merciful as thou art merciful!"

11. But, alas, it grieves me to look upon the multitudes immersed in sensuality, enslaved to covetousness, or by constant dissipation become incapable of thought. "They regard not the operations of thy hands." Created by thy power, they say not, "where is God our maker?" Maintained by thy providence, and "loaded with thy benefits," they pay thee no tribute, "neither are they thankful." The beasts of the field and the

fowls of the air have more feeling than they.
"The ox knoweth his owner, and the ass his
master's crib: but they do not know, they
do not consider." The lark that mounts toward heaven, with implicit gratitude chant-
ing thy praise, the birds that sing among the
branches, straining in sweet emulation to
warble forth the joy with which thou hast
inspired them, upbraid those sons and daughters of men who neglect to join in the sym-
phony. Father of spirits, awaken them to
reason, and to duty. Show them the empti-
ness of sin, and the wisdom of religion. Oh,
persuade them that those alone are in the
path of happiness, who seek it in glorifying
thee, in doing good, and retiring, when they
may, from the vanities of life, to contemplate
in sacred solitude and manifestations of divine
perfection.

12. How truly delightful to break away
from clamor, confusion, and discord, into a
calm retreat, and there to harmonize with
nature, and with thee her God! What relief
to the burdened and pensive mind, there to
drop its cares, to shake off for a while those
anxious thoughts that too often entangle and
depress it, and "as with the wings of an eagle
to mount up" to the serene region of pious
hope and self-enjoyment, from thence to look
down upon the lessening world, to pity the

distraction of its lovers, and triumph in the portion of the righteous!

13. From privileges like these, O Lord, thy servants return to the offices of social virtue with renewed activity and vigor, acquire a greater superiority to the temptations of their state, and are armed to meet its difficulties and dangers with firmer resolution. Thus I read in thy holy word, that when the pious and benevolent labors of the day were past, "Jesus went up into a mountain apart to pray." And thus it was, that by conversing with thee, remote from interruption, and nearer to thy seat of majesty in that sublime retirement, his soul derived new strength, lay open to the fullest emanations of thy paternal favor, and glowed with fresh ardor of zeal and charity to go about doing good, to teach, to suffer, and to die for mankind.

14. But, O my Father and my God, where shall I find language or conceptions adequate to thy inestimable love, in the redemption of the world by Jesus Christ, that last and brightest discovery of thy attributes, that divinest object of human or angelic study? Here, indeed, all my faculties are swallowed up in wonder, veneration, and joy. Here my heart is overwhelmed with speechless humility and thankfulness; and while I adore in silence this unequaled mystery, I would "behold in

it, as in a glass, thy glory''; till by its transforming power I am ''changed into the same image,'' prepared to ''see thee as thou art,'' and, through the intercession of my Savior, received to the contemplations of heaven. AMEN.

A Prayer of Ashton Oxenden

O thou, whose name is love, who never turnest away from the cry of thy needy children, give ear to my prayer this morning. Make this a day of blessing to me, and make me a blessing to others. Keep all evil away from me. Preserve me from outward transgression and from secret sin. Help me to control my temper. May I check the first risings of anger or sullenness. If I meet with unkindness or ill-treatment, give me that charity which suffereth long and beareth all things. Make me kind and gentle toward all, loving even those who love me not. Let me live this day as if it were to be my last. O my God, show me the path that thou wouldst have me to follow. May I take no step that is not ordered by thee, and go nowhere except thou, Lord, go with me. AMEN.

A Prayer From the Coptic Liturgy of St. Basil

Lord, our God, great, eternal, wonderful in glory, who keepest covenant and promises for those that love thee with their whole heart; who art the life of all, the help of those that flee unto thee, the hope of those who cry unto thee; cleanse us from our sins, secret and open, and from every thought displeasing to thy goodness—cleanse our bodies and souls, our hearts and consciences, that with a pure heart and a clear soul, with perfect love and calm hope, we may venture confidently and fearlessly to pray unto thee. AMEN.

A Prayer of William Bright

O most loving Father, who willest us to give thanks for all things, to dread nothing but the loss of thee, and to cast all our care on thee who carest for us; preserve us from faithless fears and worldly anxieties, and grant that no clouds of this mortal life may hide from us the light of that love which is immortal and which thou hast manifested unto us in thy Son, Jesus Christ our Lord. AMEN.

SELECTIONS FROM
The Hidden Life of the Soul

BY

JEAN NICOLAS GROU

JEAN NICOLAS GROU

French theologian, born at Calais November 24, 1731; died December 13, 1803. "I write nothing of myself," he says, "God directs my pen; I often take it up, not knowing what I am about to say, and sometimes I marvel at the thoughts suggested to me. If God gives me *'de quoi'* I write freely; if not, I wait his will." Grou was not only a theologian but a classical student of a humble and childlike spirit. "The outer life of a really devout man," he says, "should be thoroughly attractive to others." He worked in classical as well as theological lines. An example of the latter is his "Traité dogmatique de la vraie religion"; for the former, he translated Plato's "Republic," "Laws," and some of the "Dialogues."

The Foundations of the Hidden Life

God has given us the "law of perfect liberty," to the end that we should use it to his service; and that liberty is never so safe as when we trust it unreservedly to him, setting self-will aside, and leaving all to him: "for we know that all things work together for good to them that love God." Self-rule will probably err. Moreover, those who choose their own path must be responsible for the consequences thereof, however serious; whereas when God rules, we need nothing save patient trust. He loves us far more than we can love ourselves, and he watches over us with more than a Father's love. Trust in him, and it is impossible for devil or man to hinder his grace.

All peace and happiness in this world depend upon unreserved self-oblation to God. If this be hearty and entire, the result will be an unfailing, ever-increasing happiness, which nothing can disturb. There is no real happiness in this life, save that which is the result of a peaceful heart; and Holy Scripture tells us that "there is no peace to the wicked." Even religious people who only

By kind permission of Longmans Green & Co.

half give themselves up to God know but
feebly what this peace is; they are easily dis-
turbed by many things, scruples, dread of
God's judgments, or the changes and chances
of life. But the soul which gives itself wholly
and without reserve to God, is filled with his
own peace; and inasmuch as we are prone to
grow like that to which we are closely united,
the closer we draw to our God so much the
stronger and more stedfast and more tranquil
shall we become. Those who cleave to the
things of this world are for ever tossed about
with the waves and storms of uncertainty—
God alone is immovable, unchangeable, and
he who trusts in him will never be confounded.

Of our own strength we are equally incapable of doing good either in great works or
small, but it is safest to aim at the lesser,
leaving God to call us to serve him in greater
things when he may see fit. Meanwhile, little
things come daily, hourly, within our reach,
and they are not less calculated to set forward our growth in holiness than are the
greater occasions which occur but rarely; indeed in some ways we may turn them to more
profit, inasmuch as they do not war against
humility, or tend to feed self-deceit. Moreover, fidelity in trifles, and an earnest seeking
to please God in little matters, is a test of
real devotion and love. It is quite possible

to perform very ordinary actions with so high
an intention as to serve God therein better
than in far more important things done with
a less pure intention. Surely it needs but to
meditate upon the holy household of Nazareth
to realize this truth, while God's own Word
tells us that "he who despiseth little things,
shall fall by little and little." Let your aim
be to please our dear Lord perfectly in little
things, and to attain a spirit of childlike
simplicity and dependence.

One great hindrance to growth in God's
love is self-love. It is chiefly thereby that
Satan gets a hold over us; and all human
respect, the fatal snare of so many souls,
springs from no other source. All God's dealings with those whom he leads in the hidden
paths of the spiritual life tend to root out
self-love; as, on the other hand, all our difficulties and inward struggles arise from it.
In proportion as self-love and self-confidence
are weakened, and our will bowed to that of
God, so will hindrances disappear, the internal troubles and contests which harassed
the soul vanish, and it will be filled with peace
and tranquility. But it is well to bear in
mind that as we advance in the spiritual life,
our self-love is apt to change in character,
becoming more refined and subtle, and consequently more treacherous and harder to

uproot. In truth, we can only perceive this dangerous enemy by the help of God's own light, which reveals the secrets of the heart; and he only shows us our danger by degrees, giving us the means at the same time of overcoming it. Thus we seldom realize the force of self-love until God's dealings are tearing it out of our hearts; and then if we cooperate with his grace, his love will speedily fill the vacant place, until by degrees the whole soul is his only. Then, indeed, that soul realizes the promised blessing of the "pure in heart" —and "shall see God." Such a soul may suffer, but it will suffer joyfully, unresistingly, and no sufferings can take away that peace of which Jesus said, "My peace I give you: not as the world giveth, give I unto you."

It will be profitable to review the various degrees of the spiritual life, and to trace how God deals with our self-love in each. Of course the most obvious form is a sensuous love of self, and a clinging to sensible and material pleasures. God draws his servants from these by filling them with heavenly delights and consolations, beside which earthly enjoyments grow pale and worthless. Next, self-love cleaves to these very consolations, this tangible delight and satisfaction, and then God gently withdraws external delight, without depriving the soul of peace and rest-

fulness. But when self-love begins to rely
upon this peace, then again he permits that
to be troubled, and the soul loses all self-
resource, all self-confidence. At times, too, the
devil tempts the struggling soul with impure
thoughts or lurking doubts, under the pressure of which it is hard to believe that we are
not consenting to the evil one. It may be
that the strength of such temptations increases, while we seem to ourselves capable
of less and less resistance; we are aghast at the
sight of our own sinfulness, and imagine that
God must reject us; self-love finds no rest for
the sole of its foot, and scarce knows how to
serve God for himself only, while so devoid
of all tangible comfort. This condition will
last probably until the soul learns not to think
of itself, but to dwell in God alone; and then,
indeed, self-love is conquered. God grants
a new and heavenly life to the soul which has
thus died to self—it is filled with him, united
to him. It loves, and is loved again—no more
trouble, no more fearfulness, no more temptation. Even suffering is but a fresh stimulant
to love. Such a Christian waits peacefully for
death, which will but fill up the measure of
perfect love. "Old things have passed away,
and all things become new."

As the soul advances in holiness, God's
active power within it increases, while its own

action diminishes. It is our part to still our natural restlessness, and give place to his uninterrupted workings; so that day by day our souls may lie more passively in his hand, until our will be wholly merged in his will. It must be our chief aim, having given ourselves wholly to God, to let him take possession of all that is in us. He is wont to take all that we give him, even our very moral being and free will; yet he does but accept the offering in order to restore it to us perfected beyond all that the heart of man can conceive. Even as an earthly parent might test and try the love of a favorite child, by seeming harshness, and then finding it unchangeable, would redouble his tenderness and affection, so does God deal with his children. Self-interested, calculating love, is not the ''perfect love'' which alone is worthy of God. That love knows neither limit nor measure, human prudence can not restrain it, it reaches out to ''the foolishness of the cross.'' That was the love wherewith Jesus loved us: and be sure that whatever we lose in this life for his sake, we shall win for all eternity; but what we deny him here, will be lost to us for ever hereafter.

Jean Nicolas Grou

True Devotion

By "devotion," I mean a soul devoted to God, and there can be no stronger form of expressing perfect readiness to bear and do all things for him to whom we devote ourselves. All earthly devotion (I speak only of such as is lawful and permitted of God) is necessarily limited, but there is no possible limit to our devotion to God; the moment that a shadow of reserve or hesitation slips in, it ceases to be true self-devotion.

Real devotion, then, consists in perfect readiness to do and suffer all things without exception or reserve for God's sake, and it is indeed a most choice gift of the Holy Spirit, one which we can not pray for too earnestly; and which we must never suppose ourselves to have sufficiently attained, inasmuch as we ought to keep up a perpetual growth in the gift itself, as in its fruits.

Such devotion is inward, influencing the very depths of the soul, its intention and will. It does not depend upon reason, imagination, or feeling, nor is its existence proved by a capacity for talking eloquently about divine things, or by glowing thoughts of God, nor even by sensitiveness and tears. Devotion is not a passing emotion—it is a fixt, enduring habit of mind, permeating the whole life, and shaping every action. It rests upon a conviction that God is the sole Source of holiness, and that our part is to lean upon him and be absolutely guided and governed by him; and it necessitates an abiding hold on him, a perpetual habit of listening for his voice within the heart, as of readiness to obey the dictates of that voice. Thus it is impossible to attain true devotion without an interior and recollected spirit, which is ever seeking to possess itself in peace; and those who give way to the things of sense, imagination, or passion, even in that which is lawful, will never acquire that devotion whose first work is absolute mastery over the senses, the passions, and the mind. If you will look at devotion from this point of view, you will see that he who is inquisitive, restless, busy about other men's affairs; or given to criticize and discuss his neighbors, gossiping, ill-natured, slanderous, contemptuous, proud and sensitive; or self-satisfied, opinionated, the slave of human respect, and consequently irresolute, weak and changeable—such a man, I say, can not be devout in the true sense of the word.

He who is truly devout is much given to prayer, delighting in communion with God, and ever realizing his presence—by which I do not mean that he is always consciously thinking of God, which is an impossibility here on earth; but his heart will always be united to God, and all his actions will be regulated by God's Holy Spirit. In meditation, he is not dependent upon books, or methods, or intellectual efforts, scarcely even upon those of the will: his soul need only look within, and there is God—and God's peace. At times he may feel spiritual dryness, but that peace will always be real and blessed notwithstanding. He will rejoice more in prayer which has its measure of suffering, and wherein self-love finds no resting-place, than in such as is merely an indulgence to the imagination. Such a man never seeks himself in serving God, but realizes the precept of the ''Imitation''—''Wherever you find yourself renounce yourself.'' He will strive to fulfil all the duties of the state of life to which it has pleased God to call him perfectly; as well as all the just claims of society. Faithful to his religious exercises— he is not their slave—he can interrupt, postpone, or even forsake them for a while, if need be. So long as he is not seeking his own will, he feels satisfied that he is doing God's will. He does not seek restlessly after good works, but does what his hand findeth to do, with all his might; and when he has done his very best, he is content to leave results with God. He prefers hidden good works to those that are seen and praised of men, but neither does he shun these where God's glory and his neighbor's welfare is concerned.

The really devout man does not overwhelm himself with vocal prayers and religious exercises, which leave him no breathing space. He aims at constant freedom of heart. He is neither scrupulous nor over-anxious, but moves on his daily road in simplicity and confidence. He is firmly set to refuse nothing God asks of him, to yield in no way to self-love; never to be guilty of any deliberate fault; but at the same time he does not torment and worry himself with petty vexations. If he falls into some error, he does not fret over it, but rising up with a humble spirit, he goes on his way anew rejoicing. He is never surprised at his own weakness and imperfection, neither is he discouraged by the results of such imperfection—knowing that of himself he can do nothing, through God's help, everything: he does not trust in his own good intentions and resolutions, but solely in God's grace and goodness. Were he to fall a hundred times in the day, he would not despair—he would rather cry out lovingly to God, appealing to his tender pity. The really devout man has a horror of evil, but he has a still greater love of that which is good; he is more set on doing what is right, than avoiding what is wrong. Generous, large-hearted, he is not afraid of danger in serving God, and would rather run the risk of doing his will imperfectly than not strive to serve him lest he fail in the attempt. The outer life of such a man should be thoroughly attractive to others. He would be simple, honest, straightforward, unpretending, gentle, kindly—his conversation cheerful and sensible, he would be ready to share in all blameless mirth, indulgent to all save sin.

Be certain that true devotion is never gloomy either in itself, or as regards others. How should he who is in possession of real happiness, be sad? Earthly passions—ambition, avarice, lust, these may well make a man gloomy and absorbed, and drive him into wild mirth in the vain hope of stifling his pain. But he who truly serves God will find that his service "is perfect freedom," come what may—poverty, contempt, or pain. We still daily prove the truth of St. Augustine's well-known words, "Thou hast made us for thyself, and our heart knoweth no rest until it attain to thee."

True Holiness

But few, even of those who have specially devoted their lives to God, have accurate ideas as to the character of true holiness. Most people are apt to believe that it consists in a routine of religious practises, and a diligent observance of certain externals. If, moreover, they occasionally experience some conscious religious emotions, they make no question but that they are really holy—never stopping to ascertain whether these emotions are from God or merely the action of their own hearts. Yet often such persons are liable to many faults unperceived by themselves, which it would not be easy to make them see. They may be narrow-minded, pharisaically precise in their devotions, full of self-esteem, touchy, self-conceited, obstinate, unyielding, or affected in outward manner, altogether deficient in truthfulness, simplicity, and reality; yet all the while they secretly esteem themselves more highly than other men, and they may even despise and condemn the true piety of others, which they are unable to perceive. This unreal, harsh judgment is sadly too common among Christians; but surely it is the self-same spirit which crucified our Lord Jesus Christ; and in truth it crucifies him in

his servants even to this day; for whoever
gives himself wholly to God and seeks earnestly to lead an interior life, runs a risk of draw-
ing down jealousy and criticism, perhaps
calumny and persecution, upon himself.

If you would realize perfect holiness, seek
it as set forth in Jesus Christ. He is our
only Example, and it was to give us such an
example that he took upon him the form
of man. All holiness which is not shaped and
formed upon that model is false and unacceptable to God, and if it deceives men, it can
never deceive God or win an entrance into
heaven. Be it yours to study holiness with
Jesus for your Teacher, and be not slack in
asking him for light and grace, that you may
learn his lesson perfectly.

Jesus "pleased not himself" (Rom. 15:3).
He never sought his own pleasure or gain; no
single deed of his was ever wrought with a
view to the praise of man, or that he might
shun man's wrath. God the Father, his will,
his glory, were the objects of the Savior's
every movement. "I came not to do my own
will, but the will of him that sent me." Our
great Example has taught us that holiness is
inward—it does not consist in excited evanes-
cent feelings, but in a deep, honest conviction,
which finds vent in action—in an entire sacrifice of self to God, a boundless love and

charity toward men. Such was the spirit of
the Savior's life. He fulfilled every tittle of
the law, but meanwhile he taught by word and
deed that all such observance must spring
from inward love, or it is no better than
slavish obedience. He has taught us to esteem
this life as a mere pilgrimage—a passage, a
time of probation in which our love to God
may be ripened. He "minded not earthly
things"; he taught us not to be anxious for
the morrow, but to rest wholly on his Father's
good Providence. Jesus voluntarily embraced
that life which men shrink from most, which
they seldom endure save from necessity. He
did not condemn riches, but he gave the pref-
erence to poverty. He did not condemn the
distinctions of rank and position, which are
in truth God's own appointment, but he
taught us that there is a choicer blessing, a
greater nearness to heaven, to be found in a
lowly condition; and that self-esteem, founded
on high birth, wealth, or power, is a fatal
snare. All irregular pleasures he has con-
demned, and while permitting us the use of
certain lawful enjoyments, he himself ab-
stained even from these. Prayer and the exercise of his gracious ministry filled his earthly
life—"Wist ye not that I must be about my
Father's business?"

If we may say it reverently, nothing could

be more simple, plain, or unaffected than the deeds and words of our Lord. He taught "as one having authority"; but it was lovingly, in a familiar way, without pomp or display; his miracles were often almost secret, and his apostles and evangelists were led by the Holy Spirit to record his earthly history with the same striking simplicity.

Remember, too, his tender compassions for all true penitents—"I came to call, not the righteous, but sinners to repentance." Think of his pitying goodness to the publican, to Mary Magdalene, to the Samaritan, to the woman taken in adultery; and compare it with his condemnation of the Pharisees' pride, their avarice and hypocrisy. Remember, too, how patiently he bore with the roughness and frailties of his own apostles. From our point of view, it seems as tho it must have been a sore trial to his incomparable refinement to live with those ignorant men, full of imperfections and faults as they were. Even the holiest men find no small difficulty in sanctifying their intercourse with their fellow creatures; the closer they are to God, the more gentleness, patience, and toleration they need in their dealings with those around—it is a perpetual struggle. But Jesus bore every persecution in patience, meeting every attack with truth and innocence; silent before his accusers, forgiving his murderers; shedding his blood for them. All who "seek to live a godly life must suffer persecution"—it may be through ridicule and slander, or it may be through more overt acts. Then is the time to take Jesus as an example—to bear all things in defense of the truth; to make no answer to calumny, save by a holy life; to be silent when words are not necessary; to leave our justification with God; to put aside all bitterness, all resentment; to render good for evil; to pray for those who injure us, and believe that they are but instruments working out God's will upon us. Such conduct as this is worthy to be called holy, and God seldom sends such trials until a man has been long proved and molded. Blessed are they who endure! "If ye suffer with him, ye shall also reign with him." It can only be through an altogether extraordinary grace that any one is able to accept such trials gladly, still less to desire them. Let us rather be content with our "day of small things," seeking nothing lofty for our weak puposes, but daily imploring God that no human respect may ever make us unfaithful to the duty which we owe to him.

Jean Nicolas Grou

Self=Sought Strength, and God's Strength

St Paul said "When I am weak then am I strong" (2 Cor. 12:10). That is, "When I am filled with a sense of my own weakness, and experiencing my utter helplessness, put all my confidence in God; then I am strong in the power of his might, then I can do all things through Christ which strengtheneth me" (Phil. 4:13). But on the other hand, it is no less true that when we are strong in our own conceits, we are indeed weak; when we fancy ourselves able to do and bear all things of ourselves, and glory in our strength, then is the time of utter weakness, for God withholds his support from presumption, and we are left alone.

In fact, then, our own strength is real weakness, absolute weakness, and tends to naught save humiliating falls; while conscious weakness, together with a lowly spirit of confidence in God, is true strength, God's own strength. Are you tempted to ask why God wills us to be thus conscious of our weakness? Because "his strength is made perfect in weakness"; because he is a jealous God, the beginning and end of all that is holy; and because he would not have his crea-

tures rely upon their own frail courage or
their good intentions. When in his mercy
he leads a soul in the higher paths of sanctification, he ever begins by stripping it of all
self-confidence, and to this end he allows all
our own schemes to fail, our judgment to
mislead us: we grope and totter, and make
countless mistakes, until we learn wholly to
mistrust ourselves and to put all our confidence in him. When a beginner feels the
marvelous strength of grace, and first re-
joices in the clear light of God's truth, he
not unnaturally fancies himself able to do and
suffer all things for his Lord. Nothing seems
too hard, perhaps he even craves for heavy
crosses, great humiliations, honestly believing himself able to endure them. Nor is this
presumption—arising as it does from inex-
perience and the first warm breath of grace—
displeasing to God, if the soul meanwhile be
true and simple, and free from vanity and
self-conceit. Nevertheless, he soon lowers
all such self-confidence; let him but hide his
grace for a moment, leaving the soul to itself under the most trivial temptations; and
speedily weariness and disgust come on;
difficulties unseen before spring up; the soul
fails under slight pressure; a word, a look
suffices to disturb him who had fondly believed himself capable of so great things.

Then, very likely, he falls into the opposite extreme, is discouraged and fearful, fancies that he will never achieve anything, and is tempted to cast away all his good resolutions. In truth unless God came to the rescue, he would do so.

Such trials as these are repeated, until at length the soul fully realizes its own powerlessness to do anything alone, and its need of total dependence on God. One time the trial comes in the shape of a temptation, to which we are on the point of yielding, and then God upholds us when we thought all was over with us; another time passions which we flatter ourselves were extinct, break out anew and all but overpower us; or countless lesser imperfections humble us—we feel a strange repugnance, almost a disgust, toward what is right, our prayers and religious exercises are irksome and cold. All this is God's way of humbling us in our own conceit, and teaching us that, without his grace, we are capable of all evil indeed, but wholly incapable of the smallest good deed, or hope, or thought. Then when, after many a fall, the soul has learned its lesson, and we are freed from all self-reliance, God gradually gives us his own strength, ever reminding us that it is not ours, but his only. And so we learn to bear sufferings, humiliations, toil,

and weariness for God's sake and the good
of souls; difficulties can not hinder us, dangers
can not appal us—and that because it is no
longer we who labor and suffer, but God in
us. Such a one gives him all the glory, believing himself to be but a frail instrument
in divine hands. It was in this spirit that
St. Paul enumerated all his great toils and
sufferings for the gospel, adding, "I am nothing . . . not I, but the grace of God which
was with me" (2 Cor. 12:11; 1 Cor. 15:10).
But a man must have passed through many
a fiery trial, and be dead indeed to self, before he can attain to such a point. To those
who do so attain, what is left save one cease-
less song of praise! they are one with God,
he is in them, and self has ceased to exist.

How are we to approach such blessed
strength? First of all through a stedfast
will to refuse nothing that God requires of us,
and to do nothing deliberately which can dis-
please him. Next, we must learn to take our
faults humbly, as proofs of our weakness, and
use them to increase our trust in God, and
our mistrust of self. We must be on our
guard against excitable feelings, and not
fancy ourselves stronger or better because of
them. Our true measure is what we are when
deprived of sensible grace. Neither must we
be discouraged at our own wretchedness, or

give way to the thought that we can not do or
bear any special thing; our duty is, while
confessing that of ourselves it is impossible,
to remember that God is all-powerful, and
that through him we can do whatever he may
require of us. We must learn to say with
St. Augustine, "Give me what thou com-
mandest, and command what thou wilt." We
must not marvel at our own reluctance to do
right, but rather pray earnestly to overcome
it, not taking credit to ourselves for any such
victory, but heartily thanking God for it.
Finally, we must equally avoid presumption
and cowardice; the one springs from over-
weening self-confidence, the other from imperfect confidence in God. Both alike are met
by the same remedy—a constant recollection
that he is the source of all strength. Who
can presume who knows that his strength is
in no sense his own? who despair, knowing
that God, all-powerful, all-mighty, has promised to be his strength, and his strong salvation?

The Soul's Life

[Seek ye after God, and your soul shall live.—Ps. 69 : 33.]

Herein lies the root of our duty and of all
happiness. Happiness is the soul's life; without happiness, or the hope thereof, life seems
not worth having. What is this happiness,

and how is it to be found? Holy Scripture tells us, in God only; and "our life is hid with Christ in God." Just as the body becomes a prey to corruption, when its union with the soul is dissolved, so the soul depends for life upon its union with God; yet not after a wholly selfsame manner. The body contains an inherent principle of corruption, whereas the soul has an inherent principle of life—*i.e.*, its faculty of knowledge and love. But were these to be expended on itself alone, the soul's life must inevitably deteriorate, and, as a natural consequence, it is ever reaching forth toward objects more satisfying wherein to rest. Such rest is not to be found in the things of sense; "the Spirit giveth life," and it alone; and until the soul drinks, and drinks deeply of the Spirit of God, it will not find its true life. He kindles the burning thirst which leads us to the fountain of living water, and he has promised to satisfy it abundantly; but he will have us ask before he gives, and to that end he has taught us to use the blessed force of prayer. The soul can not die in the sense of ceasing to exist, but its death consists in ceasing to know or love God; and weary indeed is that man's life who has turned away from these saving truths—to him all is restlessness and anxiety, fretting desires, unfulfilled hopes—

no peace, no light, no satisfaction. But he who has found his soul's life in God is happy —not in truth with perfect happiness; that is not granted to men in this world, but a foretaste thereof—he has a secret joy which is beyond the reach of temptation, unrest and sorrow; a quiet confidence and stedfastness which abide even while the waves and storms of life sweep over him. God has promised, not that he shall be free from crosses, rather do they form the ladder by which the soul mounts upward—but that he will abide with his faithful servant through them all, and be his Rock, his Castle, his strong Foundation. In this world he may suffer loss— "the Lord killeth and maketh alive: he bringeth down to the grave and bringeth up; the Lord maketh poor and maketh rich, he bringeth low and lifteth up" (1 Sam. 2:6, 7); but while "death worketh in us," in our senses and passions, our human spirit and will, it is "that the life of Jesus might be made manifest in us"—the life of love, of glory, of perfect happiness for the soul.

The Soul's Peace

[Great is the peace that they have who love thy law.—
Ps. 119 : 165.]

This peace will not be won by mere literal
obedience; God's law must be loved as well
as obeyed; there must be the filial spirit as
well as the legal duty rendered. Those who
obey God's law only because they fear his
judgments can not look for the overflowing
peace and joy which are the reward of a loving service; a service which confesses heartily
that his "yoke is easy, his burden light," and
which aims at promoting his glory rather than
any reward. Not that such a spirit in any
way ignores the fear of hell or the hope of
heaven, but it is raised to something beyond
them both. When the soul has sincerely
given itself up to God, he fills it with his
own peace, a peace which makes all earthly
things indifferent—as before his presence, ab-
sorbing the heart. It is our strength, our
comfort, our guide; the deeper and more con-
firmed it becomes, the greater our spiritual
perfection; so that in truth to obtain and
preserve this peace is the real secret of the
interior life. There are a few simple rules
which may help the soul in this blessed
work.

And, first, enjoy such peace as you do the gift of health, without constantly examining into it. If you were to be always feeling your pulse to see whether you were well or ill, you would probably end by making yourself ill; and it is equally unwise to be for ever gaging the soul's peace. It is easy to confuse real peace with what is a mere matter of feeling. In the earlier stages peace brings great conscious sweetness, but this may pass away without any real loss; just as after a severe illness, we are alive to each degree of returning strength, and when fully restored to health, we do not notice what is habitual to us. Next, try to act with simplicity, not thinking overmuch about your actions, either present or past; all anxious self-searching is hurtful to peace. If your conscience does not reproach you, it is needless to cross-question it; it is enough that you give diligent heed when its whispers are heard, and a perpetual self-torture and questioning as to whether your intentions are right or wrong tends to nothing save perplexity and restlessness. Be sure that vague general fears are rather the work of your imagination than of God or your conscience. Fears that you have not said all you ought in confession, that you did not explain yourself properly, that your contrition was imperfect, that you did not re-

ceive holy communion with fitting disposi-
tions, and the like vague fretting apprehensions, are not of God. When he stirs the soul
to fear that it has sinned, it is always with
a clear definite reproach; you must learn to
despise and set aside those self-dissections.
Again, bear in mind that God never casts the
soul into trouble and anxiety when it is truly
seeking him. He warns, he rebukes, but he
never troubles you; he enables you to see
your fault, to repent and make amends, but
it is all done calmly—restlessness and anxiety
are the devil's work, and to be withstood.
Moreover, it is a most important point never
to change your spiritual course because of
any such troubles: prayer, communions, all
your devotional exercises must be persevered
in, and you will ere long conquer Satan and
regain peace. Another great help in the attainment of peace, setting aside as that does
the delusions of self-love, is to follow the ad-
vice of some spiritual guide. Above all, beware of letting go the spirit of peace because
of your faults. Humble yourself before God
because of them, repent, make such amends
for them as you are able, and then do not
dwell upon them any more. It is often mere
pride which frets at finding itself beset by
the same often renewed faults, and at its lack
of spiritual progress. Do not deceive your-

self into the belief that such disquiet is humility. A really humble soul accepts its faults with patience, and goes on afresh in confidence and hope.

A Prayer of Henry Alford

O Lord, succor, we beseech thee, us who are tempted. May nothing induce us to distrust thy care over us, nor to use thy gifts to the denial of thee, their giver. May we never presume upon thy protection when we are forsaking thy paths, and tempting thee. May we never, for the sake of any supposed gain or advancement, quench the testimony of thy spirit, or prove disloyal to thy service. Do thou so support us in all temptations that, when we have been tried, we may receive the crown of life, which thou hast prepared for them that love thee. AMEN.

A Prayer From the Gallican Sacramentary

Give me, O Lord, purity of lips, a clean and innocent heart, humility, fortitude, patience. Give me the spirit of wisdom and understanding, the spirit of counsel and strength, the spirit of knowledge and godliness, and of thy fear. Make me ever to seek thy face with all my heart, all my soul, all my mind; grant me to have a contrite and humble heart in thy presence. Most high, eternal, and ineffable Wisdom, drive away from me the darkness of blindness and ignorance; most high and eternal Strength, deliver me; most high and eternal Light, illuminate me; most high and infinite Mercy, have mercy on me. AMEN.

A Prayer of Eugene Bersier

O thou who art Love, and who seest all the suffering, injustice and misery which reign in this world, have pity, we implore thee, on the work of thy hands. Look mercifully upon the poor, the opprest, and all who are heavy laden with error, labor, and sorrow. Fill our hearts with deep compassion for those who suffer, and hasten the coming of thy kingdom and justice and truth. AMEN.

SELECTIONS FROM

Hours of Christian Devotion

BY

FRIEDRICH AUGUST GOTTREU THOLUCK, D.D.

FRIEDRICH AUGUST GOTTREU THOLUCK

German theologian and preacher, was born at Breslau, March 30, 1799; died at Halle, June 10, 1877. Attended the gymnasium of his native city and the university of Berlin. In 1821 he was graduated as licentiate of theology, and became privat-docent; in 1824 he was appointed extraordinary professor of oriental literature. In 1826 he went to Halle as ordinary professor of theology, which position he occupied till his death, with the exception of a brief period (1827-29) spent in Rome as chaplain of the Prussian embassy. His principal works are "Die Lehre von der sünde und dem Versöhner, oder die wahre Weihe des Zweiflers" (Berlin, 1823, Eng. transl., "The Doctrine of Sin and the Propitiator," London, 1836); Blüthensamnlung aus der morgenländischen Mystik," (1825); "Commentary on Romans" (1825; Eng. transl., Edinburgh, 1834); on "John's Gospel" (Hamburg, 1827; Eng. Transl. Edinburgh, 1836); on "Sermon on the Mount" (1835; Eng. transl., 1834-37); on "Hebrews" (1836; Eng. transl., Edinburgh, 1842); and on "Psalms" (1843; Eng. transl., Philadelphia, 1858); "Die Glaubwürdigkeit der evangelischen Geschichte" (1837); "Stunden christlichen Andacht" (1840; Eng. transl., "Hours of Devotion," London, 1853); "Light from the Cross, Sermons on the Passion of our Lord" (Philadelphia, 1858); "Miscellaneous Essays" (1839); "Lutherische Theologen Wittenbergs in 17. Jahrhundert" (Hamburg, 1852); "Das akademische Leben des 17. Jahrhundert" (Hamburg, 1852, 1854); "Geschichte des Rationalismus" (part 1., Berlin, 1865, never finished). A complete edition of his works appeared in 1863-72, in 11 vols.

God Is the Chief Good

God is the great epitome of light;
If thou wouldst nothing lack, possess him quite

How the Soul Is Taught By Heavenly Wisdom to Pray

I

THE SOUL: Oh Lord, I long to pray to thee aright. Wilt not thou thyself instruct me how to do it?

HEAVENLY WISDOM: Tell me, my child, why thou desirest to pray to me? Is it for my sake or thine own?—is it to laud and praise me, or to crave some boon for thyself?

THE SOUL: Lord, thy question perplexes and puts me to shame. But the purpose of it is to bring to light what is in man. Thou art my chief and eternal good, and well I know that I ought to pray, and give thee thanks and praise, solely for thy sake. And yet there is something for which I have a keen and perpetual desire, and which I passionately long to obtain from thee by my prayers.

HEAVENLY WISDOM: And what is it on

119

which thou has thus set thy heart above all measure?

THE SOUL: Lord, it is to know for certain that, after this life in time, I shall enjoy a blessed eternity in thy presence.

HEAVENLY WISDOM: And why, O soul, is thy desire for heavenly blessedness so keen?

THE SOUL: Lord, it is, as thou knowest, because this earth, with all its good things, can not fully satisfy me.

HEAVENLY WISDOM: Well, then, thou shalt obtain the boon on which thy heart is so fondly set. I shall command the chief of my heavenly ministers to apportion to thee the treasures of paradise, and shall rejoice to hear that my heaven can give what my little earth was too poor to supply.

THE SOUL: Hear this, dost thou say? Methought that it was in thy presence O Love eternal, that I was to enjoy the delights of heaven; but how can even heaven be heaven to me, if I do not find thee there?

HEAVENLY WISDOM: What good, O soul, can it do thee to have my presence at thy enjoyments? Have I not promised thee my gifts, and was it not for these that thou didst desire to pray to me? Surely thou art asking too much.

THE SOUL: O Lord, thou knowest my inmost heart. It was before thy face, and only there, that I thought of enjoying thy good things; but if my joy be not also thine, and thy joy mine, even thy paradise can not content me.

HEAVENLY WISDOM: Well, then, if thou canst not be happy without me, art thou willing to have me, even tho I bring thee no gifts at all?

THE SOUL: Lord, thou leadest me into temptation; but I reflect, and still I answer; "Whom have I in heaven but thee? and there is none upon earth that I desire beside thee" (Ps. 73:25). Yet, if I have found favor in thy sight, permit me still further to ask a question.

HEAVENLY WISDOM: Say on, my son; I wish to know all that is in thy heart.

THE SOUL: Whilst thou were speaking, a blessed light arose within me, and now I know what thou art. Art thou not so transcendently great a good, that if I were only to possess thee, I should possess all the other things which I wish to have—wisdom, and peace, and love, and beauty, and rest?

HEAVENLY WISDOM: Thou hast spoken well. I am indeed the shield of the righteous, and their exceeding great reward (Gen. 15:1). And now I understand what it is which thou didst wish to obtain by thy prayers. Tell me, then, if in asking me to teach thee how to pray, thy purpose was to thank and praise me, or rather, to obtain me as a boon to thyself.

THE SOUL: Again thou art pleased to lead me into temptation. Why dost thou ask that question? Is not my love all that thou carest for? What else but thyself dost thou give us in thy gifts? and how can a creature laud and praise thee more than by making thee the boon for which he craves?

HEAVENLY WISDOM: My son, thou sayest what is right, but mark the delusion in which thou wert entangled. When intending, in thy prayers, to laud and praise me as the chief good, it yet was not myself but my gifts that were the object of thy desire.

II

THE SOUL: Lord, thou art to me so high and precious a good, that henceforth I will no longer pray for any earthly good, at all, but solely for thyself.

THE LORD: 'Tis well, my son. The portion thou needest of the good things of earth will be given to thee by him into whose hand they are committed.

THE SOUL: How shall I understand thee, Lord? Is there, then, any other hand but thine own into which good things are committed?

THE LORD: No, my son, mine is the hand from which all the good things both of earth and heaven are received. Why, then, wilt thou not ask from me the earthly ones, nor thank me for them? Methought I was so dear to thee that thou wouldst accept of no gift unless it came from a Father's hand. Methought that, on that account, all my gifts would seem to thee to be fraught with blessing. When I presented thee with an earthly good, did I not mean by it, no less than by my spiritual gifts, to attest to thee the continuance of my love? And dost thou value an attestation of my love at so low a rate?

THE SOUL: Lord, now that thou showest it to me, I see how foolishly I spake. It was, however, only that my whole endeavor might be aimed with a single eye at thyself, that I wanted not to have my thoughts diverted by any perishable object, and therefore meant no longer to pray to thee for earthly blessings.

THE LORD: Dear soul, thou sayest thou didst not wish to distract thy mind by looking at transitory things, but observe how thou didst divide thy heart; for didst thou not intend to praise me for what my heaven bestows, but to be dumb for every boon that my earth confers?

THE SOUL: Lord, thou puttest me to shame. In my desire to be simple-minded I have erred in my own wisdom, and become double-minded. As thou art the Lord of heaven, and no less also the Lord of earth, I no doubt ought to ask, and likewise thank thee, for earthly blessings. Forgive me for what I said in my folly; but, inasmuch as I have taken upon me to speak unto thee, and fear that my heart may cleave to created things, I now entreat that thou wouldst thyself teach me the right way to pray for earthly blessings.

THE LORD: My son, thou hast said that there is none in heaven or earth whom thou desirest more than me, and that I am thy chief and eternal good. If, then, that be true, I will show thee the way to pray for earthly blessings, and yet to have thy heart wholly detached from them. Thou didst strive with ardent desire to reach my heart; strive therefore after every blessing I bestow, as if it were a path by which my heart may be reached.

THE SOUL: Full well I know that the spiritual influences, emanating so blissfully from thee are nothing but beams of light, intended to guide us back to the sun whence they came. But with thy permission I would ask if this be also the case with earthly blessings?

August Gottreu Tholuck

THE LORD: Didst thou ever, at the rising of the sun, observe how its image is reflected, as if it were a miniature sun, in every drop of dew? Such is the relation between my divinity and all this earthly creation. In none of the creatures oughtest thou to enjoy anything save what is gentle, and sweet, and lovely; and whatever is gentle, and sweet and lovely, in any created thing, is my signature and mark. On the contrary, all that is harsh, and hateful, and bitter, belongs to the creature itself. And so, my child, you see how, from every created thing upon the earth, there is a way to the heart of my Godhead.

THE SOUL: I do see it; but be not angry with me if I once again open my mouth, for there is still something which is strange in my eyes. If every created thing be a way to thy heart, how comes it that thy manner has always been to impoverish the most pious of thy servants here below more than all others, altho they are most accustomed to read thy signature and mark; while, on the other hand, thou lavishest the good things of earth on those who are far from thee?

THE LORD: For no other cause or reason, dear son, save that I am the Lord, and have ordered all things in weight, number, and measure. As the signature and mark which I impress upon terrestrial blessings are written in large letters, legible even to the simple, it is to the simple that in my wisdom I have allotted terrestrial blessings. But as my wisdom has inscribed a better signature, altho in fainter lines, upon poverty and privation, these are the boons I have reserved for them who are the "children of the secret."

THE SOUL: "A word fitly spoken is like apples of gold in dishes of silver" (Prov. 25: 11). Lord, this is a hard saying, but thy Spirit will be to me a light within.

Teach Us to Number Our Days

There's nothing that we less can trust
　　Than life and all it gives;
Nothing more sure than that to dust
　　Returns whatever lives.
By every step in life's brief race,
　　From life itself we part;
Joy dies within the heart apace,
　　And with it dies the heart.

[If after the manner of men I have fought with beasts at Ephesus, what advantageth it me, if the dead rise not? Let us eat and drink; for to-morrow we die.—I Cor. 15: 32. This saying of a Greek poet shows the view taken of life by many of the heathen who did not believe in the world to come.]

[It is appointed unto men once to die, but after this the judgment.—Heb. 9: 27.]

[So teach us to number our days, that we may apply our hearts unto wisdom.—Ps. 90: 12.]

August Gottreu Tholuck

May it not be said of the vast majority of mankind that they live as if they imagined they were never to die? And yet it is not so. The fact seems rather to be that, aware how short is the span that separates them from the confine at which they must surrender and bid adieu to all this earth has given them, they would fain enjoy life while it lasts. "Death makes pale the face," is indeed a weighty truth; but it fares no better than all other such weighty truths when committed to the power of man. If, in the hand of one, it becomes a staff on which he safely leans, in that of another it is transformed into a serpent. Does death indeed, he says, make pale the face? "Well, then, come on, let us enjoy the good things that are present; and let us diligently use the creatures like as in youth. . . . Let us crown ourselves with rosebuds ere they be withered" (Wisd. of Sol. 2 : 6-8).

But what is this pale death, for on that all depends? Is it the black wall at which the pilgrim halts, and—goes down? Is it the sleep which no dreams disturb? Or is it the dark partition between us and the holy land? Is it the swift moment, the little bridge, on which the brief sleep of time encounters the long awakening of eternity? That black is the wall at which the days of our life terminate is denied by none. Well for him who can discern in it the little door through which the light of the day of judgment throws its purple rays!

Judging by what meets the eye, we might suppose that altho the leaves of that door stand always open, the vast majority of mankind had never observed it. Like Belshazzar, they appear to sit at the banquet of life without one thought of the dark and silent hand which is all the while inscribing upon the wall, "Thou art weighed in the balance and found wanting." I am persuaded, however, that this is mere appearance. I am confident that there is not a human being whose heart has not, some time or other, felt a presentiment of the terrors of judgment. No one believes that all is over at death, or at least believes it firmly and at all times. And will not what is to ensue thereafter merely resume the thread which was broken here; and if so, will there be no accusers to testify of hours misspent, of privileges abused, of places profaned, of debts unpaid, and hidden secrets of iniquity?

If there be no presentiment of a day of judgment even in the heart of the thoughtless, whence comes their dread of being left alone? This feeling admits of no explanation but the fact that even here on earth there are ac-

cusers which, in solitary hours, present to
man his unpaid accounts. Or whence, if not
from such a presentiment, come the resolutions which so many form, and repeat, and
again repeat, to amend their lives and seek
out new paths for their feet? Oh that the
ability were only as strong as the wish! but

> At thirty, man suspects himself a fool;
> Knows it at forty, and reforms his plan;
> At fifty, chides his impotent delay,
> Pushes his prudent purpose to resolve—
> In all the magnanimity of thought,
> Resolves and re-resolves, and dies the same.

It is true that serious thoughts like that of
the day of judgment do not float upon the
surface, and this may be the reason why many
a one appears far less concerned than he
really is. Let some man of God, however,
push the probe deep into the thoughtless
heart, and it is soon seen that he touches the
quick. No one probably perceived from the
countenance of Felix, the Roman governor,
that any dread of eternity lingered in his
greedy and voluptuous bosom. But if that
had not been the case, why do we read that,
"as Paul reasoned of righteousness, temperance, and judgment to come, Felix trembled,
and answered, Go thy way for this time"
(Acts 24:25).

Yes; without a doubt, in the deep despondency which creeps over us all at the thought of separation from the good things of this life, there is always some touch of the terrors of eternity.

> Begin the song of death to sing,
> That solemn parting strain;
> Perhaps this very day may bring
> An end to all thy pain.

Yes; without a doubt, the awe which these words inspire springs not merely from solicitude about what we leave behind, but likewise from anxiety about what awaits us before. No one can be happy in this present life unless he be assured of salvation in the life to come. In former days, when as yet I knew not in what I believed, it used deeply to affect and humble me, while composing long dissertations upon such questions as, whether the soul is immortal, and what immortality is—to hear believing Christians speaking upon the subject as confidently as if they had just come from the heavenly land. This was nothing but the fulfilment of the promise, "He that believeth on the Son hath everlasting life," and "tasteth the powers of the world to come."

As for thee, man, who has never yet made his peace with God, how can he possibly be happy in his life, seeing that every moment is conducting him farther and farther away from the place which contains all that gives pleasure to his heart? Every tick of the clock, every particle of sand that drops in the hour-glass, proclaims that a fragment of his life, and, with it, of his fortitude and joy, is gone. Dost thou hear the low but mournful lay which the softly falling grains never cease to sing?—

Behold, O man! and thee bethink
How these, our little sands, that sink,
Life's ebb proclaim.

As one by one we steal away,
So silently does fell decay
Prey on thy frame.

What though our course be still and slow?
No pause by day or night we know,
But ever drop.

And come there will an hour when all
Are gone, and as the last shall fall
Thy pulse shall stop.

O my soul! is it indeed the case that no man can be happy in this life without the assurances of salvation in the life to come? Be it then thy endeavor so to live as at the hour of death thou wilt wish to have lived. While time lasts, lay hold on eternity. Above all, lay hold on him who has said, "Whosoever believeth on me hath everlasting life."

Suffer Little Children to Come Unto Me

> Thou sayest, the babe is mine,
>   I'll train him as I list;
> But, sure, ere he was thine,
>   He appertained to Christ.
> And wilt thou not a charge so dear,
>   For him who lent it to thee, rear?

[Lo, children are an heritage of the Lord: and the fruit of the womb is his reward.—Ps. 127 : 3.]

[Suffer little children, and forbid them not, to come unto me; for of such is the kingdom of heaven.—Matt 19 : 14.]

[Ye fathers, provoke not your children to wrath; but bring them up in the nurture and admonition of the Lord.—Eph. 6 : 4.]

"Many children make many prayers, and many prayers bring much blessing." Yes, verily, when we reflect how highly God must esteem the man to whom he gives children, we see that there ought to be no end of prayer and supplication and thanksgiving. That he has sent children into a house is of itself a sufficient reason for him to send his blessing, too. To give existence and life is a work which the Divine Majesty has usually reserved to himself. What, then, shall we think of giving existence and life to an immortal being made in the divine image! How dreadful that so excellent a grace is by men contaminated with sin, so high a prerogative dishonored in the service of lust! If mere existence in this present world is of no worth, unless the present world become a training-school for the world to come, how audacious to bestow an earthly existence upon a human spirit without a serious purpose, formed in the sight of God, of training it for heaven! He commits a wrong who becomes a father and does not at the same time undertake the sacred duty of rearing his child for eternity.

What the Lord has affirmed concerning them ought to be enough of itself to make the care of the young one of the holiest occupations in life. Once when the twelve were disputing with each other which of them should be the greatest, he took a child and set him in the midst of them: and when he had taken him in his arms, he said unto them: "Whosoever shall receive one of such children in my name, receiveth me: and whosoever shall receive me, receiveth not me, but him that sent me" (Mark 9:36, 37). On another occasion he put his hands on the children, and prayed and said: "Suffer little chilren, and forbid them not, to come unto me: for of such is the kingdom of heaven" (Matt. 19:14). "Verily I say unto you, whosoever shall not receive the kingdom of God as a little child shall in no wise enter therein" (Luke 18:17). No doubt some who pretend to be masters of Scripture have wrongly interpreted these sayings, inferring from them that the Lord

looked upon little children as being in all
respects spotless and perfect, like the blessed
angels in heaven; but it is said that Adam
begat children "in his own likeness, after his
image" (Gen. 5:3), and in Adam the image
of God was then defaced. If the Lord have
set them up as a pattern to us in one respect,
he has not done so in all, and Paul writes:
"Brethren, be not children in understanding" (1 Cor. 14:20). What the Lord loved
in the little ones was, their knowing so well
that they can not stand upon their own feet,
but must seek wisdom and strength and welfare at their mother's bosom. Of a like disposition were the persons whom he enlisted in
his service, and only such as these have ad-
mission into the kingdom of heaven. Not a
few interpreters suppose that he spake also
of children when he said, "Whoso shall offend one of these little ones which believe
in me, it were better for him that a millstone
were hanged about his neck, and that he
were drowned in the depth of the sea" (Matt.
18:6); and again, in a subsequent verse—
"Take heed that ye despise not one of these
little ones; for I say unto you, that in heaven
their angels do always behold the face of my
Father which is in heaven" (Matt. 18:10).
In my opinion, however, when he so spake, he
had in his eye those of his disciples who pos-

sest a childlike frame of mind, and who clung to his breast as children do to a mother's for he specifies "one of these little ones which believe in me." Inasmuch, however, as such disciples have the same disposition spiritually which little children have naturally, it may doubtless be said that they belong to the same family, and that therefore it ought not to be forbidden to apply to the one what has been affirmed of the other.

According, therefore, to the word of Christ himself, the jewel in the souls of children is the sacred trustfulness with which they look to their parents for strength and counsel and help; and what he desires is, that they who love him should repose in him a similar trust, and such a trust for certain he will never deceive. Is it possible, then, that any parents who are leaning on the bosom of the Savior with the same reliance with which their children lean upon theirs, and who are constrained to confess that he never gave them a stone when they asked for bread—is it possible, I repeat, that such parents can ever prevail upon themselves to give to their children in place of bread a stone, and in place of a fish a serpent? Oh no, is the answer from the heart of every father and every mother. Oh no, they cry, and yet they do it. For this, in fact, is done by all who leave untutored, or at least without the nurture and admonition of the Lord, the early age when children cling to parents with absolute confidence, and ever seek to catch their eyes, as if imploring, do you guide us, for we can not guide ourselves. What else is the eye of your child constantly directed to yours, and confidently endeavoring to read what he ought to do, but a perpetual petition to the effect, Give, Oh, give me spiritual bread? And when, in place of giving them that, you leave them without the nurture and admonition of the Lord, or any direction as to the way in which they ought to go, you really give them what the Scripture calls "offense," meaning by the term an occasion of temptation and fall? And think what the Lord has said respecting those who offend a youthful soul, whether it be a disciple or a child. He has said, that to be drowned in the lowest depths of the sea, which was the severest punishment inflicted upon criminals in this present world, would still be light when compared with that which is reserved for them in the world to come. Alas! it would be impossible to number the parents and teachers who, according to this saying, would certainly perish, were there not comfort in the thought that they know not what they do.

It goes to one's heart to see a young tree

which, while still slender and soft, might have been trained to grow straight and bear fruit, and show a beautiful head, abandoned instead as a prey to insects of every kind, and left exposed to injuries of the weather and the rough hand of the forest thief. It is a terribly earnest saying, that to corrupt a child is as great a crime as to seduce a maid. Yes, for the souls of children are virgin souls; and if the angels, who see the face of God, are not ashamed to minister to them, how can men, how can you who are parents and teachers, be negligent in such a service? In fact, if it be right to speak of meriting a divine reward, there is no merit so enviable as that of saving a soul of a child. The noblest of all missions is into the world of youth. This is the field which yields the increase of an hundredfold.

Now, what we require to give to children we must ourselves first of all possess. The least of such gifts is daily bread, and with respect to it man is not worse off than the beast of the field and the fowl of the air. Kin cleaves to kin, and the tree does not disown its own fruit.

> Poor though she be, a mother's arm
> Will shield her babe from cold and harm

And so parents take thought for the daily

bread of their children and provide it, not merely for the present, but even for the future. Here, however, the devil lays for them a special snare; for in how many cases do we find that a niggardly spirit enters the house along with the children? But if there be truth in Luther's saying, that God, who is rich, allots to every child committed to a parent an inheritance of its own, into possession of which it infallibly comes, whether the parents live or die, prosper in the world or come to poverty—why wilt thou not rather say to thy children as Luther did to his, "I do not leave you riches, but I leave you a rich God"? How large soever may be the treasures which, by scrimping from morn to night, you may accumulate for your children, they will be a far smaller fortune than if you bequeathed to them a true and simple and sincere faith in the rich God of heaven.

The next thing which children are entitled to receive from parents is education and training for the station of life to which they are called. If it be true that next to the wife of his heart a man can find no greater good upon earth than a profession which he loves, and if this be a matter upon which parents have to decide for their children, how great the responsibility which it involves! What is it, then, that generally determines the choice which parents make? It is a serious attention to the voice of God, uttering itself in the circumstances and outward relations, but most of all in the capacity of the child? Alas! in how many cases is it not caprice, or unbelieving parsimony, or ostentation, or conceit, which decide the point? How many have been thrown into a false career by the mere whim of having the son take the father's place? How many by infidel niggardness which insisted on seeing before it would trust, and how many more by pride? There is truth in the proverb—

> Pity the man who takes in hand
> The task he does not understand,
> And what he could do lets alone—
> No wonder he is soon undone.

Many have thus been shipwrecked, and frequently has it been the parent's fault. And yet, when the powers and capacities of the youth prove insufficient for the calling into which he was forced solely by their conceit, how often do they, in place of condemning themselves, revile God, and cry out that nature had neglected and been a stepmother to their child! whereas you yourselves have been the stepmothers, and would not listen to God's voice, who never meant your son to be an instrument for accomplishing great and mighty things. You grieve when your infant, in place of being hale and sound, comes into the world a cripple, and you would deem it the height of cruelty to make a cripple of him yourselves; and yet, ye proud and unbelieving parents, in the vanity that consumes you, make your children cripples in mind! For just as an instrument is put out of shape when pushed into a case which does not fit it, so may a man's whole nature be crippled and distorted when he is forced into a profession for which God never designed him. By such conduct foolish parents sin against their children, whose minds they deform; against God, to whose voice they do not listen; and against their fellow men, who are defrauded of the benefit of talents which might otherwise have profitably ministered to them.

The chief and peculiar gift, however, due by parents to children, is the nurture of the inner man and tuition in the word of God. It is written, ''The Lord said, Shall I hide from Abraham that thing which I do; seeing that Abraham shall surely become a great and mighty nation, and all the nations of the earth shall be blessed in him? For I know him, that he will command his children and his household after him, and they shall keep the way of the Lord, to do justice and judgment'' (Gen. 18:17-19). So highly did

God esteem in his servant Abraham the bringing up of his children in piety! In this way, by the mere education of their offspring, may parents earn for themselves heaven or hell. In the passage where the apostle says of the woman, "Notwithstanding she shall be saved in child-bearing, if they continue in faith and charity and holiness with sobriety" (1 Tim. 2:15), he does not speak merely of bringing children into the world, but of what that implies, *viz.*, their upbringing and tuition; for he supposes that the mother herself continues in the faith, and, as a consequence, also understands the right way of bringing them up. Yes, fathers and mothers, to no teacher in the whole world has the task of making Christians of your children been made so easy as to you; for if confidence is a stretched-out hand, toward whom is the hand of a child stretched out more than toward his parents? You would count it a crime to offer them, when they are hungry and ask of you earthly bread, nothing at all, or perhaps a stone; and would it be no crime if, when they held out their hand for spiritual bread, you were to give them nothing or, what is worse than nothing, falsehood in place of truth? Recollect that the worldly and skeptical spirit has not as yet interposed its bar, so that in the breast of a child holy truths may be lodged and take root so firmly that no wind of doubt or worldly pleasure shall be able to extirpate them. The season of childhood, however, passes away, and is succeeded by one in which there are no longer open doors in the mind for faith to enter. You must not, however, merely teach religion, you must show it to your children, and make your life their school-book. Of a truth the child who in seasons of deep affliction has learned from the example of his father or mother what it is to pray, will never in after years, even tho he may deviate very far from the path of truth, entertain a mean opinion of the power of prayer. At a more advanced stage of life he may make the acquaintance of pious men, but then doubts of their sincerity will always intrude. If, however, a child, until he has reached a riper age, has in his father's house witnessed the fear of God pervading, controlling, and animating all that was done, never more will he be able to doubt that piety is a great blessing and a truth. With whatever violence skeptical theories may assail him, still, just as no one can be brought by the most subtle arguments to doubt the reality of the material world around him, so no one who in his childhood has been privileged to gaze into the paradise of a pious life, can ever doubt its existence; whereas he who has not yet entered it may hear it so depreciated and absurdly spoken of that he will never enter it at all.

Beware, ye who are parents, of harsh severity; but beware, also, of lax indulgence; "It is God's will," as Luther tells us, "that we should honor him in two ways—the one, by loving him as a Father on account of the benefits he has bestowed or will bestow; the other, by fearing him as a Judge, who has punished us already and will do so again. For this reason it is that by the mouth of the prophet he says: 'If, then, I be a Father, where is my love? and if I be a Master, where is my fear?' (Mal. 1:6). Fathers are an image of God; and being both fathers and masters of their children, they ought to be both loved and feared." In former days, no doubt, it was too much the practise of fathers to govern by fear, especially among the heathen, where they exercised the right of putting their children to death. And it is for this reason that the apostle addresses to fathers, who were of heathen origin, the special exhortation "not to provoke their children to wrath" (Eph. 6:4; Col. 3:21). To the same purpose Luther also says: "The child that has once been intimidated and disheartened is rendered useless for everything, and fears and trembles whatever he is called upon to do or attempt; and what is worse, if timidity have been allowed to take hold of his mind in childhood, there will be difficulty in rooting it out in his whole after-life; for as he was wont to quake at every word of father and mother, he will continue to tremble at the rustling of a leaf.'' In another passage he also says, ''Children ought not to be too severely beaten. My father once beat me so severely that I fled from his sight, and sulked at him until he used means to reconcile me.'' Often, too, have pious parents gone astray by attempting to force the piety of their children by legal means, enjoining upon them prayer, and reading the Bible, and going to church, too exclusively as mere external works, and not reflecting that the piety of the young can not wear the same serious face as that of the old. In this way they have embittered the cheerful sports of their boys and girls, and so hindered them, when grown up to be young men and women, from acquiring any experience of the world. A piety that had thus been made to wear a rueful countenance in youth has often been followed by a feeble and spiritless manhood, or has broken out into knavery in after years. Upon this subject, likewise, Luther, who was so great a foe to all hypocrisy, has beautifully said: ''Here we have a king for our school-

master, and an excellent one he is. He does
not forbid the young to go into company, or
indulge in mirth, as the monks do with their
disciples. In that case they would grow up
mere dolts and blockheads, as even Anselm,
who was the parent of monachism, has told
us. For he says that a youth so tackled and
secluded from society is like a fine young tree,
which might have borne fruit had it not been
planted in a pot. Monks imprisoned the
young like birds in a cage, and thereby pre-
vented them from seeing or hearing or talking with other persons. It is, however, dangerous for them to be thus left alone and cut
off from society. They ought, on the contrary,
to be allowed to hear and see and acquaint
themselves with all manner of persons and
things, in such sort, however, as to be kept
in moderation and decency. Nothing is
gained by monastic restraint. It is good for
a young man to be much in company, provided
at the same time he be trained up in integrity
and virtue, and withheld from vice. The
tyrannical constraint of monks is altogether
hurtful; for mirth and amusements are as
needful to youths as meat and drink, and are
likewise the means of keeping them in
health."

On the other hand, this age of ours has
grown so soft and maidenish that it will no

longer suffer the rod to be used to children.
According to the words of Luther, "False
natural affection blinds parents to such a degree, that they care more for the flesh than
for the souls of their offspring. It is, however, of the highest necessity that every parent shall pay a far greater and deeper and
more constant attention to the soul of his
child than to the flesh, which has been derived
from himself; and that he shall look upon
him in no other light than as a costly and immortal treasure committed by God to his care,
in order that it may be neither stolen nor
destroyed by the devil or the flesh." The
wise man of old has said that "he that spareth
his rod hateth his son; but he that loveth him
chasteneth him betimes" (Prov. 13:24).
"Thou shalt beat him with the rod, and shalt
deliver his soul from hell" (Prov. 23:14).
And the son of Sirach says: "Cocker thy
child, and he shall make thee afraid; play
with him, and he will bring thee to heaviness;
laugh not with him, lest thou have sorrow
with him, and lest thou gnash thy teeth in the
end. Give him no liberty in his youth, and
wink not at his follies. Bow down his neck
while he is young, and beat him on the sides
while he is a child, lest he wax stubborn, and
be disobedient unto thee, and so brings sorrow to thine heart" (Ecclus. 30:9-12). No

doubt it is better if the end can be gained without the use of the rod, for the human being has received from God an intelligent mind, and is capable of affection and confidence; and the preferable way is to begin when he is young to govern him by the feelings of his heart. Naturally, however, children are more affected by impressions made upon the senses than by reasons addrest to the understanding, and it is also profitable and right to employ such impressions in aid of the word of exhortation. Besides it accustoms the child to understand what retribution is. The mere enticements of love and kindness in the hands of the heavenly Father sometimes fail of success with us, who are his perverse children, and so it behoves him to have the rod always ready as well as the sweetmeats; and far less shall we be able to forego the use of it toward our children.

As soon, then, as a parent observes that being always good to his child is no longer doing the child good, he ought in all that relates to God and good morals wholly to forget that the child is his own flesh and blood, and to recollect that he, to whom the right to punish belongs, has put the rod into the hands of parents as well as of magistrates, and that it is their duty to use it—not, indeed, in the ebullition of carnal passion, but in the name and for the service of the Most High. A great emperor, Frederick II, once said, "I have sometimes repented of my severity, but never of my clemency." There is, however, reason to fear that in these days our parents will have to say the very contrary. A good intention is now thought to make so many things good, and yet it can never falsify what experience has proved, that "Well intended is oft lamented." Be persuaded, then, O parents! not to follow so much the inclinations of your heart, but rather the admonitions of Holy Scripture, and in the training of the young prefer the word and the law of God to all the suggestions of your own mind.

Dear Master, if life is to go well with us who are advanced in years, vouchsafe once more true piety to our youth. The Christian Church is now using great exertion in the way of sending the gospel by missions to the heathen, and that, also, is a work consistent with thy holy will and commandment; but do thou on that account all the more stir up among us who tarry at home a warm zeal to institute missions without number among the young. Abroad thy servants have much to do before they succeed in gaining the love and confidence of the heathen, and inducing them to inquire after the way of salvation; whereas our children affectionately look up with eager eyes, expecting to receive from us the bread of life. Yes, verily, if the man who aspires to be a preacher would but consider how many useful sermons he might preach by conversing more frequently with the little ones, and implanting divine truth more largely in their hearts, the kingdom of God might be built up among us much more effectually than has ever yet been done. Gracious God, incline thy heart to our children; take upon thyself the training of them, and make of them a holy nation, whose sacrifice of love and obedience may put to shame those who have grown to manhood and old age. Thy word declares that "out of the mouths of babes and sucklings thou hast perfected praise"; fill, then, their mouths with thy praise, and mold them to be new foundation stones for thy spiritual Zion.

A Prayer From St. James Liturgy

O God, the Father of our Savior Jesus Christ, whose name is great, whose nature is blissful, whose goodness is inexhaustible, God and Ruler of all things, who are blessed forever; before whom stand thousands and thousands, and ten thousand times ten thousand, the host of holy angels and archangels; sanctify, O Lord, our souls and bodies and spirits, search our consciences, and cast out of us every evil thought, every base desire, all envy and pride, all wrath and anger, and all that is contrary to thy holy will. And grant us, O Lord, Lover of men, with a pure heart and contrite soul, to call upon thee, our holy God and Father who art in heaven. AMEN.

SELECTIONS FROM

The Still Hour

BY

AUSTIN PHELPS

AUSTIN PHELPS

American clergyman and author; born at West
Brookfield, Mass., January 7, 1820; died at Bar
Harbor, Me., October 13, 1890. He graduated
at the University of Pennsylvania in 1837, and
studied at Andover and Union Theological Semin-
aries; was pastor of Pine Street Congregational
Church Boston, 1842-48, and professor of sacred
rhetoric at Andover Theological Seminary, 1848-
79, and president from 1869. Among his writings
are: "The Still Hour" (Boston, 1859); "Hymns
and Choirs" (Andover, 1860); "The New Birth"
(Boston, 1867); "Sabbath Hours" (1870);
"Studies of the Old Testament" (1879); "The
Theory of Preaching" (1881); "Men and Books"
(1882); "My Portfolio" (1882); "English Style"
(1883); "My Study" (1885); and "My Note
Book" (1890).

one who is familiar with those phases of religious experience which are so often the

152

Absence of God In Prayer

[Oh that I knew where I might find him.—Job 23 : 3.]

"If God had not said, 'Blessed are those that hunger,' I know not what could keep weak Christians from sinking in despair. Many times, all I can do is to complain that I want him, and wish to recover him."

Bishop Hall, in uttering this lament two centuries and a half ago, only echoed the wail which had come down through living hearts from the patriarch whose story is the oldest known literature in any language. A consciousness of the absence of God is one of the standard incidents of religious life. Even when the forms of devotion are observed conscientiously, the sense of the presence of God, as an invisible friend whose society is a joy, is by no means unintermittent.

The truth of this will not be questioned by one who is familiar with those phases of religious experience which are so often the burden of Christian confession. In no single feature of "inner life," probably, is the experience of many minds less satisfactory to them than in this. They seem to themselves in prayer to have little, if any, effluent emotion. They can speak of little in their devotional life that seems to them like life; of little that appears like the communion of a living soul with a living God. Are there not many "closet hours" in which the chief feeling of the worshiper is an opprest consciousness of the absence of reality from his own exercises? He has no words which are, as George Herbert says, "heart deep." He not only experiences no ecstasy, but no joy, no peace, no repose. He has no sense of being at home with God. The stillness of the hour is the stillness of a dead calm at sea. The heart rocks monotonously on the surface of the great thoughts of God, of Christ, of eternity, of heaven—

> As idle as a painted ship
> Upon a painted ocean.

Such experiences in prayer are often startling in the contrast with those of certain Christians, whose communion with God, as the hints of it are recorded in their biographies, seems to realize, in actual being, the Scriptural conception of a life which is hid with Christ in God.

We read of Payson that his mind, at times, almost lost its sense of the external world in the ineffable thought of God's glory, which rolled like a sea of light around him, at the throne of grace.

We read of Cowper, that, in one of the few lucid hours of his religious life such was the experience of God's presence which he enjoyed in prayer that, as he tells us, he thought he should have died with joy, if special strength had not been imparted to him to bear the disclosure.

We read of one of the Tennents that, on one occasion when he was engaged in secret devotion, so overpowering was the revelation of God which opened upon his soul, and with augmenting intensity of effulgence as he prayed, that at length he recoiled from the intolerable joy as from a pain, and besought God to withhold from him further manifestations of his glory. He said, "Shall thy servant see thee and live?"

We read of the "sweet hours" which Edwards enjoyed "on the banks of Hudson's River, in secret converse with God," and hear his own description of the inward sense of Christ which at times came into his heart, which he "knows not how to express otherwise than by a calm, sweet abstraction of soul from all the concerns of this world; and sometimes a kind of vision . . . of being alone in the mountains, or some solitary wilderness, far from all mankind, sweetly conversing with Christ and rapt and swallowed up in God."

We read of such instances of the fruits of prayer, in the blessedness of the suppliant, and are we not reminded by them of the transfiguration of our Lord, of whom we read, "As he prayed, the fashion of his countenance was altered, and his raiment became white and glistering?" Who of us is not opprest by the contrast between such an experience and his own? Does not the cry of the patriarch come unbidden to our lips, "Oh that I knew where I might find him?"

Much of even the ordinary language of Christians, respecting the joy of communion with God—language which is stereotyped in our dialect of prayer—many can not honestly apply to the history of their own minds. A calm, fearless self-examination finds no counterpart to it in anything they have ever known. In the view of an honest conscience, it is not the vernacular speech of their experience. As compared with the joy which such language indicates, prayer is, in all that they know of it, a dull duty. Perhaps the characteristic of the feelings of many about it is exprest in the single fact that it is to them a duty as distinct from a privilege. It is a duty which, they can not deny, is often uninviting, even irksome.

If some of us should attempt to define the advantage we derive from a performance of the duty, we might be surprized, perhaps shocked, as one after another of the folds of a deceived heart should be taken off, at the discovery of the littleness of the residuum, in an honest judgment of ourselves. Why did we pray this morning? Do we often derive any other profit from prayer than that of satisfying convictions of conscience, of which we could not rid ourselves if we wished to do so, and which will not permit us to be at ease with ourselves if all forms of prayer are abandoned? Perhaps even so slight a thing as the pain of resistance to the momentum of a habit will be found to be the most distinct reason we can honestly give for having prayed yesterday or to-day.

There may be periods, also, when the experiences of the closet enables some of us to understand that maniacal cry of Cowper, when his friends requested him to prepare some hymns for the Olney collection. "How can you ask of me such a service? I seem to myself to be banished to a remoteness from God's presence, in comparison with which the distance from East to West is vicinity, is cohesion."

If such language is too strong to be truthful to the common experience of the class of professing Christians to which those whom it represents belong, many will still discern in it, as an expression of joylessness in prayer, a sufficient approximation to their own experience to awaken interest in some thoughts upon the causes of a want of enjoyment in prayer.

The evil of such an experience in prayer is too obvious to need illustration. If any light can be thrown upon the causes of it, there is no man living, whatever may be his religious state, who has not an interest in making it the theme of inquiry. "Never any more wonder," says an old writer, "that men pray so seldom. For there are very few that feel the relish, and are enticed with the deliciousness, and refreshed with the comforts, and acquainted with the secrets of a holy prayer." Yet, who is it that has said, "I will make them joyful in my house of prayer?"

Distrust In Prayer

[What profit should we have if we pray unto him?— Job 21 : 15.]

The great majority of us have little faith in prayer. This is one of those causes which may produce a habit of mind in devotion resembling that of impenitent prayer, and yet distinguishable from it and coexistent, often, with some degree of genuine piety. Christians often have little faith in prayer as a power in real life. They do not embrace cordially, in feeling as well as in theory, the truth which underlies the entire Scriptural conception and illustration of prayer, that it is literally, actually, positively, effectually, a means of power.

Singular as it may appear, the fact is indisputable that Christian practise is often at a discount by the side of heathen habits of devotion. Heathen prayer, whatever else it is or is not, is a reality in the heathen idea. A pagan suppliant has faith in prayer as he understands it. Groveling as his notion of it is, such as it is he means it. He trusts it as an instrument of power. He expects to accomplish something by praying.

When Ethelred, the Saxon king of Northumberland, invaded Wales and was about to give battle to the Britons, he observed near the enemy a host of unarmed men. He inquired who they were, and what they were doing. He was told that they were monks of Bangor, praying for the success of their countrymen. "Then," said the heathen prince, "they have begun the fight against us; attack them first."

So any unperverted mind will conceive of the Scriptural idea of prayer as that of one of the most downright, sturdy realities in the universe. Right in the heart of God's plan of government it is lodged as a power. Amidst the conflicts which are going on in the evolution of that plan it stands as a power. Into all the intricacies of divine working and the mysteries of divine decree it reaches out silently as a power. In the mind of God, we may be assured, the conception of prayer is no fiction, whatever man may think of it.

It has, and God has determined that it should have, a positive and an appreciable influence in directing the course of a human life. It is, and God has purposed that it should be, a link of connection between human mind and divine mind, by which, through his infinite condescension, we may actually move his will. It is, and God has decreed that it should be, a power in the universe as distinct, as real, as natural, and as uniform as the power of gravitation, or of light, or of electricity. A man may use it as trustingly and as soberly as he would use either of these. It is as truly the dictate of good sense that a man should expect to achieve something by praying as it is that he should expect to achieve something by a telescope, or the mariner's compass, or the electric telegraph.

This intense practicalness characterizes the Scriptural ideal of prayer. The Scriptures make it a reality and not a reverie. They never bury it in the notion of a poetic or philosophic contemplation of God. They do not merge it in the mental fiction of prayer by action in any other or all other duties of life. They have not concealed the facts of prayer beneath the mystery of prayer. The Scriptural utterances on the subject of prayer admit of no reduction of tone and confusion of sense as men often put forth in imitating them. Up on the level of inspired thought, prayer is prayer—a distinct, unique, elemental power in the spiritual universe, as pervasive and as constant as the great occult powers of nature.

The want of trust in this Scriptural ideal of prayer often neutralizes it, even in the experience of a Christian. The result can not be otherwise. It lies in the nature of mind.

Observe, for a moment, the philosophy of this. Mind is so made that it needs the hope of gaining an object as an inducement to effort. Even so simple an effort as that involved in the utterance of desire no man will make persistently with no hope of gaining an object. Despair of an object is speechless. So, if you wish to enjoy prayer, you must first form to yourself such a theory of prayer —or, if you do not consciously form it, you must have it—and then you must cherish such trust in it as a reality, that you shall feel the force of an object in prayer. No mind can feel that it has an object in praying except in such degree as it appreciates the Scriptural view of prayer as a genuine thing.

Our conviction on this point must be as definite and as fixt as our trust in the evidence of our senses. It must become as natural to us to obey one as the other. If we suffer our faith to drop down from the lofty conception of prayer as having a lodgment in the very counsels of God by which the universe is swayed, the plain practicalness of prayer as the Scriptures teach it, and as prophets and apostles and our Lord himself performed it, drops proportionately; and in that proportion, our motive to prayer dwindles. Of necessity, then, our devotions become spiritless. We can not obey such faith in prayer with any more heart than a man who is afflicted with double vision can feel in obeying the evidence of his eyes. Our supplications can not under the impulse of such a faith go, as one has exprest it, "in a right line to God." They become circuitous, timid, heartless. They may so degenerate as to be offensive, "like the reekings of the Dead Sea."

Eternal Life

BY

ANTHONY W. THOROLD, D.D.

ANTHONY WILSON THOROLD

Bishop of the Church of England, born at Hougham, England. June 13, 1825; died at Winchester July 25, 1895. He was educated at Queen's College, Oxford (B.A., 1847; M.A., 1850; D.D., 1877); ordained deacon, 1849; priest, 1850; at Holy Trinity, Marylebone, 1854-57; rector of St. Giles-in-the-Fields, London, 1857-67; minister of Curzon Chapel, Mayfair, 1868-69; vicar and rural dean of St. Pancras, London, 1869-74; resident canon of York, 1874-77; bishop of Rochester, 1877-90; and of Winchester, 1890-95. He was also examining chaplain to the Archbishop of York for a number of years ranging about 1874; and select preacher at Oxford, 1878-80. He was the author of "The Presence of Christ" (London, 1869); "The Gospel of Christ" (1881); "The Claim of Christ on the Young" (1882); "The Yoke of Christ in the Duties and Circumstances of life" (1883); "Questions of Faith and Duty" (1892); "The Tenderness of Christ" (1894); and a volume of sermons, "The Gospel of Work," included in "Preachers of the Age" (1891.)

Eternal Life

[Bishop Thorold's work consists of a series of six meditative chapters built upon an interpretation of Ps. 23. He regards the "Good Shepherd" of Christ's parable as identical with the "shepherd" of this psalm. The other chapters have the following heads: Christian Assurance, Divine Providence, Chastisement, The Table of God, and The Valley of the Shadow of Death.]

[Surely goodness and mercy shall follow me all the days of my life: and I will dwell in the house of the Lord forever.—Ps. 23:6.]

Thankfulness is one of the most attractive qualities of the Christian character. While it invigorates and animates ourselves, it glorifies God and it edifies our neighbor. No doubt it has much to do with natural temperament, sound health, sufficient means, and congenial employment. Nevertheless, it is sometimes perfectly independent of these accidental causes; and he who in poverty, or sickness, or solitude, can preserve a merry heart and a cheerful countenance is a benefactor to society, a testimony to his God, and the best of all possible friends to himself.

But if thankfulness is an attractive quality of the Christian character, it ought also, within certain limits and with certain exceptions, to be a universal one. Clouds will sometimes prevent our seeing the sunshine; and every one now and then is tempted to exclaim, out of a deprest heart, "O my God, my soul is cast down within me" (Ps. 42:6). Still it may be safely asserted that the prevailing temper of a truly Christian mind is a lively sense of the divine goodness; and at the end of life, as the departing pilgrim looks back on the way by which the Lord his God has led him through the wilderness, the one exclamation of wondering gladness is, "How good God has been to me!" the one conviction of assured faith is, "He will never change. He will continue to love me to the end."

But why is this so? What is it that throws this steady and sunny light both on past and on future—that eases burdens heavy enough to crush other men—that interprets all God's dealings, even the hardest and the darkest, under the unfailing purpose of eternal love? It is the blessed knowledge of what God has been, is, and will be, to us; it is the knowing in whom we have believed, and that he is able to keep that which we have committed unto him against that day; it is the sanctifying presence of the indwelling Comforter; in a word, it is the consciousness of possessing eternal life, through abiding in the Father and the Son.

That we have eternal life now in a true, tho of course limited, degree, can be proved from many passages of Scripture. There are our Lord's words, when, about the death of Lazarus, he said to Mary, "He that liveth and believeth in me shall never die" (John 11:26); and again, on the eve of his own passion, when, in prayer to his Father, he said, "This is life eternal, that they might know thee the only true God, and Jesus Christ, whom thou hast sent" (John 17:3). There are St. Paul's words, "Set your affections on things above, not on things on the earth. For ye are dead, and your life is hid with Christ in God" (Col. 3:1, 2). There are St. John's words, "He that hath the Son hath life; and he that hath not the Son of God hath not life" (I John 5:12). The believing soul, in the language of the same apostle, has already passed from death unto life through the power of the regenerating Spirit, tho that life can not be completed or enjoyed in the full fruition of its blessedness until, in the resurrection of the body, we enter on the entire and incorruptible immortality of our whole being.

No great ingenuity is required to trace, all through the twenty-third psalm (nay, it might almost be said, through each separate verse of it) some distinct truth about this eternal life. There is the substance of it in our personal spiritual union with the Lord

Jesus. The Lord is my shepherd, belonging to me, and I to him; he dwelling in me, and I in him. The manifestation of this life is in the personal holiness of the believer, whom the Good Shepherd ever strives to lead on into the green pastures and still waters of an ever riper knowledge and fuller image of himself. Would we know how to ascertain whether this eternal life is ours or not, the answer will not be found in sudden emotions of feeling, however animating they may be; nor in a clear and consistent theological system, blessed as it is for those who have attained it; nor in aptness of controversy, useful as it sometimes is in contending for the truth; nor in an unhealthy eagerness about means of grace, which, tho they are channels of Christ's presence, are not Christ himself; —but in a life hidden with Christ in God, yet manifesting itself daily by a continual bringing forth of the fruits of the Spirit. The discipline of it is in the wisely alternating visitations of joy and sorrow according to the needs and circumstances of each individual soul.

For this eternal life extends its purifying and exalting influence over the entire being of man. It lays hold of his understanding, enabling it rightly to appreciate and humbly receive the great mysteries of the gospel, in

the Father's eternal purpose, and in the aton-
ing blood of the Incarnate Son, and the regenerating grace of the Spirit. It seizes the
heart, and strikes its roots all down it and
through it, engaging and occupying the affections for God himself, whose is the first and
rightful claim. The conscience it purges
from dead works to serve the living God
(Heb. 9 : 14), giving it rest and peace through
the precious blood that can alone wash out sin.
The will it subdues into captivity to God's
will, not by taking it away, nor by immers-
ing it in God's, as some mystics have delighted
to say, but by training and educating it into
a free and complete and cheerful and intelligent obedience. And while over the entire
moral and spiritual being of man it sheds its
blessed and increasing influence, it makes our
very mortal bodies, through the operations of
our wills and affections, servants and instruments of righteousness unto God.

But what is the method of this? The shedding forth of the love of God into our hearts
by the Holy Ghost. For observe the result
in David's mind of this spirit of thankfulness,
and the unfailing evidence of eternal life in
the soul. It is devoutness. "I will dwell in
the house of the Lord forever." God's goodness did not harden him into indifference,
nor produce in him a sense of independence

of God or of confidence in his own prosperity.
Rather it made him feel more than ever his
need of God, and that God was his only sufficient and abiding portion; that the nearer
he could live to him, the more often he could
worship him; the more he could hear of his
truth and receive of his grace, the better it
must be for him, both here and hereafter.
Nor is this the solitary expression of his feeling, since again and again in his psalms—such
as the 27th, the 42nd, and the 84th—do we
find the same.

Now, it is deeply important for us to inquire very seriously what are the chief aids
to devoutness among Christian people, and
how we may best remove the obstacles and
hindrances to it wherever such are found to
exist.

The meaning of devoutness is personal,
adoring, filial love to God the Father, as
revealed in his Son Jesus Christ. It is not,
in the usual acceptation of the word, the in-
variable accompaniment of living faith in the
soul; for there are many sincere and excellent persons, walking in the fear of God and
in the light of conscience, of whom to speak
as devout would be to describe them inac-
curately, if not altogether untruly. It is by
no means always found in company with a
great amount of accurate doctrinal knowl-

edge; for it was when Mary Magdalene was weeping over her lost Lord, whom she thought to be stolen and could not believe to be risen, that her Savior, recognizing her devoutness, rewarded it by the revelation of himself. It may be called the enthusiasm of personal religion, springing from a fervent and affectionate nature, going out after God and cleaving to him and delighting in him, not so much for what he gives as for what he is; prizing above all his gifts the constant sense of his sanctifying presence, desiring above all his graces the power of loving him more as he deserves. In David's own words, it is "thirst for God, for the living God," longing to go and appear before God; it is also the deep, unutterable adoration of a soul that throbs and burns with the very fire of heaven, the emotion of a heart that would multiply itself a hundredfold only to give all to him.

Jesus, the very thought of thee
  With sweetness fills the breast;
But sweeter far thy face to see,
  And in thy presence rest.

Tongue never spake, ear never heard,
  Never from heart o'erflow'd
A dearer name, a sweeter word,
  Than Jesus, Son of God.

If devoutness is rare, so much rarer than it ought to be, the reason is not hard to find. For we love our God with such a thin, feeble, meager, circumspect love, not in the least because he denies us the power of loving him or refuses to pour into our heart his love to us; but partly because we do not sufficiently appreciate the duty and the blessedness of loving him; partly because we hinder the outcoming of his love to us and the upgoing of our love to him, by sloth or sin; partly, also, because we do not fulfil the conditions, and use with such languor and indifference the aids and helps by which alone love to God can burn in the soul with a steady and bright flame.

If that considerable number of professing Christians who are continually lamenting their want of love to Christ and God would really and thoroughly search their hearts about it, some of them might discover that they have already as much of God's love as they have any right to expect; and that the amount which they feel to possess, whether of a sense of his love to them or theirs to him, is, as a matter of fact, in exact proportion to their real efforts after it. To be safe is practically the end and aim with which tens of thousands of professing Christians sit down in an ignoble contentedness. Not to be punished for sin, not to be shut out of heaven, not to be refused the comfortable persuasion of peace with God, not to be left knocking at the door of God's mercy uncertain if we shall ever be let in—this is what too many people look upon as the goal of the Christian's race, and the substance of his assurance, and the reward of his faith, and the pledge of his victory. Whereas it is but the starting-point, and not the conclusion; the earnest, but not the fulfilment, of his salvation. To be delivered from sin in the love and power of it is really of far more importance, both for God and us, than that we should be set free from the fear of hell, essential as that is to the liberty and cheerfulness of our service; and to be made fit for heaven is the only possible condition on which we could enjoy its blessedness, or mix in its society, or do its works, or adore its Lord. It is no doubt a most blessed thing to feel safe; yet certainly it is neither the loftiest nor the most elevating sentiment even of human nature: and to rest content with our sense of safety, comparatively indifferent to the glory or the kingdom of him who has saved us, is to fall very short indeed of our Redeemer's purpose for us, is to know nothing of the spirit of the apostle, whose one constraining motive, both of gratitude and obedience, was love to him who died and rose again.

So many of us have such a miserably low standard! We hardly care for God's love, except for the mental excitement of feeling it. We hardly care for his glory, except just so far as our personal instrumentality is concerned in advancing it. We hardly care for his presence, save when no other consolations are forthcoming. Nine out of every ten human beings are naturally disposed to be intensely idle. And this idleness creeps over the renewed nature, and lulls it into drowsiness and sloth. We are often too idle for the effort of sustained prayer. We are often too idle steadily and thoughtfully to study our Bibles. We are often too idle to interest ourseves in bearing the burdens or healing the sorrows of those around us. We are often too idle for anything much more than listening to rousing sermons, and occasionally attending a meeting for missions, and—being "scarcely saved." Unbelief is at the root of it. If we really believed that God, of, and by, and in himself, could make us happy; if we could learn to trust him, and be content with him, apart from his gifts, in the deep conviction that he is more and better than them all; if, in our jealousy for his honor, and in our appreciation of his character, and in our sympathy with his purposes, and in our gratitude for his cross, we could come to have more of his mind about sin, more to understand his intense hatred and horror of it, more, with him, to pity and yearn over the lost, more to perceive and know that the very greatest loss a human being can suffer is the loss of his image and presence, I do think we should more cheerfully and readily cast ourselves into his arms, and yield ourselves to his purposes; we should say more continually, more fervently, more honestly, than most of us can say now, "Do what thou wilt with me, only love me; and give me the power of loving thee in return!"

The conditions of devoutness are few, obvious, and simple. First, if God is to come to fill the heart with his sweetness and his glory, he must have it all to himself when he comes. By which I do not mean that he is jealous of the rightful and natural love which we give to and claim from each other. "He that loveth not his brother whom he hath seen, how can he love God whom he hath not seen?" (1 John 4:20). Love to man is often the shortest road to the love of God. Nor again, that he expects or demands perfection while we are here. But he does expect, and we must give him, sincerity of purpose in seeking him, resoluteness of will in following him, perseverence of effort in surrendering to him all we have, and all we are. Half-heartedness in religion is the true secret of the want of zeal and power in the Church of Christ; and the famous French sarcasm is sometimes almost as true of sincere, as of merely nominal, Christians, "that they have just religion enough to make them miserable, but not enough to make them happy."

Another absolutely essential condition of devoutness is the entire, and unsparing, and incessant conflict with indwelling sin, however inveterate, or pleasant, or secret from men, or indulgently treated by the world. So long as we make a truce with any sin whatever, and choose to think about it either that it is so small it does not signify, or so hidden that no one knows of it, or so powerful that we can not overcome it, just so long are we with one side of our voice inviting God to come to us, and with the other side bidding him keep away. God is a holy God; and if his servants can consent, knowingly and perseveringly, to nurse in their hearts such sins as covetousness or pride, or vanity, or envy, or evil and censorious speaking, they must take the consequences. Divine grace has a marvelous vitality, and it takes a great deal of pains quite to extinguish it. Still it is easy enough to stunt its growth; and if we are not watchful over ourselves, instead of being epistles to the Church and the world of God's

Anthony Wilson Thorold

divine power in using us as instruments of righteousness, we shall be epistles, equally well known and well read, of the power of sin to quench and smother the divine Spirit, and of the fatal certainty with which self-indulgence of any kind will, sooner or later, take its revenge on us.

Another condition of devoutness is active and continual occupation in the Lord's service. What exercise does for the body usefulness does for the soul, in quickening the circulation through the entire system, and in giving a healthy play to the organs and faculties of our being. Such occupation may be confined to the four walls of a house. It is not essential to it that it should be prominent, or varied, or arduous, or, indeed, of any special sort or kind whatever. All that is necessary is that each Christian person should feel himself a laborer in the Lord's vineyard, and should be doing with humility and cheerfulness the task the Lord gives him to do, whatever and wherever it may be. This alone (unless sickness or other cause of inability prevent it) can keep the heart awake, the will obedient, the mind ready, the conscience pure. If it involve self-denial, so much the better. Nay, the chances are, that if there is no self-denial about it, we are pleasing ourselves, instead of pleasing Christ. Some people are so constituted that they would find it harder to overcome natural diffidence in visiting the sick, or even in teaching a class of children, than to eat dry bread for a year. But to master self is the meaning of sanctification; and the sure and certain reward of following our Savior wherever he leads us is that we are thereby strengthened for the daily conflict with sloth and selfishness in our own hearts; and thus in ministering to others we are unconsciously benefiting ourselves.

Once more: it is absolutely impossible to maintain the heart in a condition of real devoutness without a steady and frequent use of those means of grace ordained and provided for us by a higher wisdom than our own, and to neglect which is both presumption and folly.

First and foremost of these is prayer—secret, frequent, sustained, and fervent prayer—prayer not only for the supply of needs, or for the sense of pardon, but for close spiritual communion with the Lord of our spirit, in at least an effort after that adoring and holy praise which is the substance of the worship in heaven. I know how hard prayer is almost at all times; how glad we sometimes feel to be able to say anything; that our best prayers ever fall short of our true aspirations; that our worst prayers are often so cold, so feeble, so poor, so wandering, they hardly deserve to be called prayers at all. And it is the humbling personal knowledge of the inadequacy and shortcomings of his own prayers that may well make a Christian writer pause, before he raises a standard that he himself so very inadequately reaches unto, as well as shrink from making a heart sad, which God would not make sad, by inviting prayer, which to many would seem so distant and so impracticable as only to reduce them to despair. Yet prayer is a habit; and the more we pray, the better we shall pray; and the highest mountain can be climbed by steady, patient walking; and if we never set a mark before us, to aim at and try for, we may soon discover that nothing is so perilous to the soul's life as contentedly sitting still. Sometimes to go to be alone with God and Christ in the fellowship of the Spirit, just for the joy and blessedness of it; to open, with reverent yet eager hands, the door into the presence chamber of the great King, and then to fall down before him, it may be, in silent adoration; our very attitude an act of homage, our merely being there, through the motive that prompts it, being the testimony of our soul's love; to have our set day-hours of close communion, with which no other friends shall interfere, and which no other occupations may interrupt, to which we learn to look forward with a living gladness, on which we look back with satisfaction and peace; this, indeed, is prayer, for its own sake, for God's sake, for our friend's sake, for the Church's sake, and for our work's sake; prayer—which we do not hurry through, to still the conscience, but which (other things permitting) we can even linger over to satisfy the heart. Oh, if we Christians, who talk so much about the privilege and blessedness of prayer, would try to avail ourselves of it more than we do, how we should reflect on the world all around us the glory, as it streams on us from the face of the Incarnate Mediator! What a power we should become to rebuke sin, and proclaim pardon, and promise liberty, and offer peace, through our continually laying hold on the hem of the garment of our glorified Lord!

There must also be a full and frequent study of God's holy Word. In holy Scripture, as Christ himself has said, we have eternal life. He is the living Word of God; the Bible is the written word. There are some persons who, without the special excuse of but little leisure, go so far as to say that the Bible is the only book that Christians ought to study, other books involving but a waste of time. It may be sufficient to reply, that to impose this as a duty on all men alike is certainly to go beyond the letter of Scripture itself; that it is hardly consistent with the reasonable and justifiable cultivation of the various mental gifts and faculties with which God has endowed us, meaning us to use them, and that we are not particularly encouraged to it by any special largeness of mental vision or Christian charity in the few individuals who observe this rule themselves. It does not, however, follow that because the Bible is not the only book for Christians to study, that they might not study it much more than they do, and with much more pains and diligence and prayer. When we open our Bibles, quite as much as when we fall on our knees, we place ourselves in God's immediate presence; and we should read his Word both in the sense of listening to his voice and with the object of discovering his will. It is quite impossible for any Christian whatever to grow in the love of God without growing in the knowledge of him. Let any one who is doubtful about it read the epistles of St. Paul's first imprisonment, and his doubts will soon disappear. But how can we grow in the knowledge of God without being much in the study of the Bible? For, first, it is the one object of the Bible to teach us the original and authoritative truth of God; and then we never appreciate truth so vividly, or receive it so gladly, or retain it so tenaciously, or impart it so intelligently, as when we have discovered it for ourselves by our own thought and effort. One hour's devotional study of Scripture will often do more than a dozen sermons to stir up in our hearts the love of God. There are many external proofs of the inspiration of the Bible. Christ's own teaching, the doctrine of his apostles, the tradition of the Jews, the universal consent of the Christian Church of all times, place the divine authority of both Old and New Testaments on a foundation which can not be moved. To let go the blessed truth of the plenary inspiration of holy Scripture, is to lose the sheet anchor of revelation, and to drift away toward the dark and restless sea of human speculation, and "science, falsely so called" (1 Tim. 6:20). But there is internal as well as external evidence of this inspiration: hundreds and thousands of simple Christians, who know nothing of argument or controversy, have discovered, through the witness of God's Spirit in their own hearts, that the Bible is the very voice of God; and there is no argument half so efficacious with the great majority of readers, for proving the divine authorship of Scripture, as the hallowing influence that the Bible itself seems to breathe over us when we bring ourselves into real contact with its contents.

Again, a great help to devoutness in this restless and distracting age is contemplation. It may be distinguished from meditation as being the attention of the mind and heart to a person rather than to a truth; and while meditation may be defined as the pondering of the spirit of some divine doctrine, with (so to speak) closed eyes and abstracted senses, contemplation is the adoring gaze of the believing and worshiping heart on the glory of its Lord and King. "Out of sight, out of mind" is a truth true in many ways. If we never set Christ himself preaching on the mountains of Galilee, dying on the cross, glorified at his Father's right hand, before our heart and imagination, we must expect only faintly to realize all that he has suffered, all that he is now doing for us; and the result will be our spiritual loss. To look on Jesus with the purified eye of faith and love, tho it may be a rare, is however, a truly blessed means of grace. There is a sense in which even now we may see, if we will, our King in his beauty; and if in the day of his return we are to be made like him in body as well as in soul through seeing him as he is, we may become spiritually like him now through contemplating his person, and meditating on his work, and pondering his character, and feeding on his words. "For, even now, we all, with open face beholding as in a glass the glory of the Lord, are changed into the same image, from glory to glory, even as by the spirit of the Lord" (2 Cor. 3:18).

There is yet one other aid toward the stirring up within us of a living devoutness to Christ, and that is, a frequent receiving of the Lord's Supper. Even in the lowest and poorest interpretation of this sacrament as nothing more than an act of commemoration of the Lord's sacrifice, one would think that nothing would be so likely to stir up our gratitude, and dispose our hearts to receive his mercy, as often to partake of the memorial of his passion; and that none of the Savior's words would be more tenderly cherished or more studiously obeyed than his dying injunction, "This do in remembrance of me" (Luke 22:19).

Now if this indeed be so—if, whenever we partake of the Lord's table in a right spirit—we feed on the very Christ himself, given to us there by the operation of his Spirit to be our meat and drink, our strength and joy, must not that blessed means of grace be especially calculated to fill us with thankfulness and self-abasement, to stir up renewed self-surrender and more habitual self-denial? And as to the objection, so frequently and not at all unreasonably, made to a frequent reception of it, on the ground of our losing blessing through a greater familiarity with it, may we not thereby be doubting, tho quite unconsciously, God's wisdom in ordaining this privilege, and mistrusting his power to prevent his ordinance falling short of his purpose to bless? Of course, it must always be a matter for individual discretion how often it may be expedient to partake of this ordinance; and while we are careful to reserve to ourselves the free exercise of our own judgment, the same liberty must be granted to our brethren. Still, it is certain that from not fully appreciating the blessedness, and apprehending the meaning, and using the opportunities, and welcoming the grace of this sacrament, some of us fall short of God's offers of blessing; for while it strengthens faith and quickens love, it also animates hope. The memorial of the cross is also the promise of the glory; and they who at the Lord's table on earth love to "show forth their Lord's death till he come" (1 Cor. 11:26) are surely more likely than others to be looking forward to the glorious moment when they will be called to sit down to the marriage supper of the Lamb.

Now, all this throws light on the eternal life in heaven, which we come to consider in the latter part of the verse, " I will dwell in the house of the Lord forever'' (Ps. 23:6). Whether David himself actually meant to refer to it is open to reasonable doubt. Certain, however, it is that he had been divinely instructed about it, and some of the most beautiful of his psalms anticipate its blessedness in language which Christians, looking back at their Lord's resurrection, can gladly and consistently use. But it is one of the features of the inspired Word that it contains depth within depth of the divine doctrine, well beneath well of the living water; and it is hardly possible for a Christian to utter these words without declaring the blessed hope of the glorious appearing (Titus 2:13) to be his own.

Heaven is spoken of here under three points of view—as a home, as a permanent home, as a home in the presence of God. It is to be a house, not a tent; a home, not a lodging; the no longer seeing through a glass darkly, but the beholding as with open face the vision of God.

Now, eternal life in heaven is plainly but a continuation and a development of eternal life on earth. It will be the same in the essence of its character, in the motive of its service, in the substance of its joys, in the nature of its glory. It will be different, for there will be no mortal body to hamper its action, no sinful nature to interrupt its progress; in perfect liberty, and in entire security, with energies that will never be exhausted, with opportunities that will never be thrown away, it will expand in the glorified soul through the eternal ages, to the praise of God and the joy of men.

The character of heaven will be the perfect unalloyed love of sinless and glorified beings. Dwelling in love, we shall, in the full sense of the word, dwell in God, and God in us. The noblest aspirations of the regenerate man will then have their full satisfaction; and if there will still be something left to wish for, if in the fulness of joy at God's right hand faith and hope shall still hold their place and fulfil their functions in the human soul, faith will be the joyful and humble sense of dependence on God and Christ, who there as here will be the spiritual food, the source of life and power to his glorified creatures, hope will vividly anticipate an ever-increasing capacity to love God as he deserves, ever-growing powers to prove and use that love in obedience to the divine will. At present it is almost impossible to conceive ourselves loving God and each other perfectly; to have every motive of service, every spring of feeling, every throb of zeal rooted and grounded in love, which self shall not spoil and pride shall not tarnish. In heaven, dwelling in an atmosphere of love, to which each contributes and of which each receives, we shall behold him who is the Sun from whom our light comes, the King from whom our royalty comes, the Priest who gives us our priesthood, the Lamb who has brought us our salvation; and the more we gaze, the more we shall love; and our growth in love will be as infinite as God.

For we can not do more than love God; there is no higher duty, and there is no greater bliss. The true idea of the character of heaven must be that of love; the only question about it is the question of degree. God is love himself: and so far as we resemble him, we shall be love likewise: and as if to show that love is worship and worship is love, the inspired account of heaven is that there shall be no temple there. Perfect love can adore and worship without signs and symbols; the Lord God Almighty and the Lamb are the temple of it (Rev. 21: 22).

Love being the character, nay, the very nature of heaven, it is clear that the service and occupation of heaven will be the simple outgoing and satisfying of that love, in whatever can serve, and please, and glorify him on whom it is bestowed. To know God's will must then be instantly and joyfully to ful-

fil it; and independently of the new means,
that may then be vouchsafed, of spiritual fellowship and of divine communications (about
which none of us can do more than guess
and speculate), we are quite sure that there
will be no moral hindrance, as there too often
is now, to ascertaining it, through our own
unwillingness to perform it when known; by
intuition we shall discover his good pleasure;
and by the unerring instinct of our nature we
shall hasten to fulfil it. For there will be
no law in heaven. Law, as St. Paul tells us,
is only for the lawless and disobedient (1 Tim.
1:6). When it is our meat and drink to
do God's will, we shall stand in no more need
of a code from Sinai. Walking in the spirit,
we shall be delivered from the letter. When
the blessed will of God is written in our hearts,
and absorbed into our wills, and apparent to
our minds, and supreme in our consciences,
we shall not want teachers to teach us, for
"all shall know me, from the least to the
greatest" (Heb. 8:11); and pains and penal-
ties will be needed no longer, when perfect
love has cast out fear.

What that service will be we can only con-
jecture, we may not presume to declare. But
death, so far as we know, can not interrupt
our spiritual existence, and will certainly be
unable to affect either our mental powers, or

our constitutional gifts, or our moral character. Nay, it is not even conceivable that the capacities we possess here, with so much to hamper their exercise, and mar their improvement, and check their progress, and disappoint their efforts, should be either suspended or diminished merely through our entrance into another state of being, which may be reasonably likened to a man's entering on mature life after the discipline and pupilage of school. We are justified, therefore, in thinking it at least probable that our service in heaven may not be altogether unconnected with our employments on earth; and that the powers and qualities, and gifts and talents entrusted to us here, will, according to the use and improvement we have made of them, decide our work and position for us in the kingdom of the Father.

For it is by no means of so much consequence what a man does as how he does it. His calling does not so much ennoble him, as he his calling. Accuracy, perseverance, conscientiousness, patience, industry are all immortal and invaluable properties of human character; and when the King comes to take account of his servants, each faithful servant's character and powers will at the end of his earthly career, come up to judgment, not for condemnation but for scrutiny; not only in reference to the past, but also to the future. Surely it is a noble and elevating reflection, one, moreover, to give much consolation and light about many otherwise unintelligible circumstances in the providential government of God, that nothing we do or suffer now that pleases God can be lost or go unrewarded and forgotten. Every man shall receive his own reward, according to his own labor (1 Cor. 3:8). Humble diligence, uncomplaining patience, cheerful self-denial, unworldly simplicity, are seen of God, if neglected by men; and tho in this world the man who takes most care of himself generally gets the best of it, in the next world he who has thought most of God and his brother will then be found the truly wise man; and in the day when God makes up his jewels to set in his Son's diadem, not necessarily those who have filled the highest places, or won the most applause, shall shine forth then with the most resplendent brightness, but those also shall be very near the throne who have postponed the praise of men to the praise of God, who have been contented to do modest duties well rather than important duties badly; whose courage has kept them poor, and whom plain-spoken honesty has deprived of advancement; who have never suffered any earthly motive to blind their eyes to the seeking of God's

glory or to blunt their hearts to the sense of
his love. There will be many widows with
their two mites set high up in the heavenly
places; and many Demases only just let in.
It will be seen then to have been better to
have had only one pound to use and to have
made two of it, than to have had five and
thrown them away.

> Be sure—no earnest work,
> Of any honest creature, howbeit weak,
> Imperfect, ill-adapted, fails so much,
> It is not gather'd as a grain of sand,
> To enlarge the sum of human action used,
> For carrying out God's end. No creature works
> So ill, observe, that therefore he's cashiered.
> The honest earnest man must stand and work;
> The woman also; otherwise she drops
> At once below the dignity of man,
> Accepting serfdom. Free men freely work.
> Whoever fears God, fears to sit at ease.
> ELIZABETH BARRETT BROWNING.

That heaven is love, is a true key to the
everlastingness of its duration. How, when
once there, we can cease to love, cease, as
has been observed already, to increase in loving, it is quite impossible to conceive. For
as there will be nothing to disappoint us in
God, so there will be nothing to tempt us in
ourselves. The more we see of God, and
learn of him, and dwell with him, the more we
must love him. His character will be in-

creasingly revealed in all its perfection, his
will in all its righteousness, his creation in
all its wisdom, his redemption in all its fulness. And if there is nothing in him to make
our song flag, or our loyalty waver, or our
love decay, or our service diminish, neither,
through his sustaining grace, shall there be
anything in us. In our glorified bodies and
in our sinless nature we shall be more than
ever the very dwelling-place of God. For
the elect in glory sin will be even impossible.
Faith shall never fail, hope shall never be
disappointed, and tho our love will never
burn with an ardor to satisfy us (for he who
thinks he loves God as much as he deserves
can hardly be said to love him at all), it
shall no longer doubt itself for its insin-
cerity or accuse itself for its lukewarmness.
That will be a glorious and an unselfish security in which the children of the resurrection shall rest themselves forever in the everlasting arms, safe in the eternal purpose of
Christ's redeeming love made perfect, and
fulfilling its own nature in teaching, and
glorifying, and elevating and beautifying all
through eternity those whom the Father has
given him out of the world.

The question of degrees in glory, incon-
testably established as it is by many passages of Scripture, is sometimes perplexing to

those who are jealous of the doctrine of salvation by grace, may be more clearly seen in the light of the undeniable fact that with all imaginable varieties of depth and power regenerate souls adore God.

As a moral question, it is simply one of justice; that justice being a revelation of God's unerring righteousness in recognizing and rewarding the use of the grace he has himself bestowed. St. Paul and the penitent thief are equally sinners saved by grace, and enter heaven on the identical terms of God's redeeming mercy; yet they shall have each their place, and their crown, and their work, and their glory, according to the fight they have fought, the course they have finished, and the faith they have maintained.

Let us look at it, however, a moment longer in connection with the idea already maintained, that the evidence of eternal life in the soul is faith working by love. Only a regenerate soul—a soul, that is, with the divine life implanted in it—can, in any real and sufficient sense, love God. As we love, we obey. And if faith receives salvation, obedience earns glory.

There are two accounts of the love of the regenerate soul; one finding it in God, the other rewarding it with God; the one proclaiming our dependence, the other vindicating our responsibility. "We love him because he first loved us" (1 John 4:19); here is the first cause of man's love to God, in God's love to man. "If any man love me, he will keep my words; and my Father will love him" (John 14:23). "I love them that love me; and those that seek me early shall find me" (Prov. 7:17), here is the growth and increase of God's love to man made dependent on man's love to God, God recognizing and rewarding the use of his own mercy by multiplying it on the faithful soul.

Now, what is glory? In the deepest sense of the word, it is the manifestation of God's image and character, shed abroad in our hearts now, as we are changed by his Spirit "from glory to glory"; to be displayed at the resurrection presently, when we shine forth as the sun and death is swallowed up in victory. But the more we love now, the more we shall love then; the nearer we live to God now, the nearer we shall be to God then; the more we deny ourselves for his sake now, the more he will recompense us then; the more we open our hearts to him and surrender our wills to him now, the more he will glorify us hereafter. And the cause of this is also the chosen instrument of fulfilling it. For nothing so expands and deepens our nature as true love, of any kind. But love to God has a special power of its own for making the heart bigger and deeper for him to come in, and inhabit it, and fill it out of his fulness. The eye of the mind being enlarged to take in his truth, more and more light shines in; the door of the heart being widened to receive his grace, God rains on it showers of blessing. The entire moral being is ever growing larger through the sanctifying influence of divine love; and thus, through the unconscious agency of his own devoutness, the Christian has "grace for grace," and yet it is "according to the measure of the gift of Christ" (Eph. 4:7). For even God can give us only according to our capacity of receiving. No vessel can be more than brimful; and tho, when once in heaven, we may all be growing alike in our power of receiving more grace, and learning more truth, and rendering more service, and drinking more joy, entering heaven we start, so to speak, with all possible varieties of moral stature and spiritual attainment—the stature and the attainments being fashioned when on earth.

Howe, in his "Blessedness of the Righteous," has a noble passage in which he contemplates innumerable multitudes of pure and happy creatures inhabiting and replenishing ample and spacious regions above, ignorant of nothing lawful, and pleasant to be known, curious to know nothing useless, endowed with a self-governing wisdom, yet with a noble freedom, all everywhere full of God, full of reverence and dutiful love, every one in his own eyes as nothing, self-consistent, ever free of all self-displeasure, all assured of their acceptance with God, all counting each other's felicity their own, and every one's enjoyment multiplied so many thousandfold as he apprehends every one as perfectly pleased and happy as himself. ...

Well may the Christian say, as he ponders these noble thoughts, "Oh, what will it be to be there!" And if the joy is so rapturous, the rest so blessed, the company so edifying, the place so glorious, Christ visible, God near, death behind, judgment over, what is our hope of this glory, and what result does it produce in us; does it strengthen us for the duties of life, and console us under its sorrows, making its losses light and its gains trifling? Surely we Christians are but half awake; and the children of this world are still in their generation wiser than the children of light. There are treasures for us that we will hardly think of, a home that it is barely worth our while to prepare for, joys which we languidly taste, gifts which we slothfully use.

Yet the night is far spent, the day is at

hand (Rom. 13:12). We have slumbered and slept till our lamps are all but gone out; let us hasten to trim them, for the Bridegroom is coming. Surely, if we quite believed about heaven all that the Bible tells us of it, how humility would clothe us, and zeal inflame us, and the thought of our inheritance ennoble us, making us calm and brave as the sons of God! We should live with men now, heirs with us of a common salvation, as those who hope presently to pass eternity together. Wherever we found souls without the divine knowledge, we should endeavor to say to them with zeal, and yet with wisdom, "Come thou with us, and we will do thee good" (Num. 10:9). We should pray, believing in prayer; we should work, for the time is short (1 Cor. 7:29); we should hate and resist sin in, at least, something of the spirit in which we shall look back at it out of paradise; sloth, and self-indulgence, and covetousness, and injustice to each other would seem even a treason against the Lord that bought us with his blood.

Oh, then, let us live for this glory, and wait for it, and do all we can to earn it, for our glory is our Master's, and he is coming to be glorified in his saints, and to be admired in all them that believe (2 Thess. 1:18). The more souls we can win for him, the more he

will see of the travail of his soul and be
satisfied (Isa. 53:11). The greater the faith
and patience that his servants manifest, the
more evident the work of his Spirit before
angels and men. It is but a very little while
we have, at the longest, in which to pray, to
trust, to suffer, to labor; and much of it is
gone already. Let us make the most of what
is left; "redeeming the time, because the days
are evil" (Eph. 5:16). And when the Good
Shepherd leads his ransomed flock to pastures ever green, and waters ever still, on the
delectable mountains of the true land of
promise, then we shall say from our hearts,
as none can quite say on this side of the river,
"In thy presence is fulness of joy; at thy
right hand there are pleasures for evermore"
(Ps. 16:11).

A Prayer of Sir Philip Sidney

All-seeing Light, and eternal Life of all
things, look upon my misery with thine eye
of mercy, and let thine infinite power vouchsafe to limit out some portion of deliverance
unto me, as unto thee shall seem most con-
venient. But yet, O my God, I yield unto
thy will, and joyfully embrace what sorrow
thou wilt have me suffer. Only thus much

let me crave of thee (let my craving, O Lord, be accepted of thee, since even that proceeds from thee)—let me crave even by the noblest title, which in my greatest affliction I may give myself, that I am thy creature, and by thy goodness (which is thyself) that thou wilt suffer some beam of thy majesty so to shine into my mind, that it may still depend confidently on thee. AMEN.

SELECTIONS FROM

My Aspirations

BY

GEORGE MATHESON, D.D.

GEORGE MATHESON

Scottish theologian and preacher (Church of Scotland); was born in Glasgow, March 27, 1842; died at North Berwick, August 28, 1906. He was educated at Glasgow University and graduated with high honors (B.A., 1861; M.A., 1862; B.D., 1866). In his twentieth year he became totally blind, but he held to his determination to enter the ministry and in 1866 was licensed to preach. His first charge was as assistant at Sandyford Church, Glasgow; then he was called to Innellan (1868-1886); and from 1886 till his retirement in 1899 at St. Bernard's, Edinburgh. Edinburgh and Aberdeen Universities conferred on him D.D. and LL.D. respectively. He was Baird lecturer 1881, and Queen Victoria invited him to preach at Balmoral 1885. He is perhaps best known by the popular hymn "O love that will not let me go," which was written at the Innellan manse in five minutes on the evening of June 6, 1882. Among his works are: "Aids to the Study of German Theology" (1874); "Growth of the Spirit of Christianity from the First Century to the Dawn of the Lutheran Era" (2 vols., 1877); "Natural Elements of Revealed Religion" (1881); "Can the Old Faith Live with the New? or, The Problem of Evolution and Revelation" (1885); "The Distinctive Messages of the Old Religions" (1892); "The Spiritual Development of St. Paul" (1890); "Studies of the Portrait of Christ" (1899-1900); "The Representative Men of the Bible" (1902-1903); and his devotional books, of which some have had an extensive sale.

Moments of Religious Solitude

[And when they were alone, he expounded all things to his disciples.—Mark 4 : 34.]

It is only when I am alone with thee that I perfectly understand thee. When thou speakest to the multitude there are many things I can not comprehend. Outward life is a parable, and it is often hard to read. I can tell the gain of my own griefs; those of my brother sometimes baffle me. Why should it not be so? My own soul is before me; the soul of my brother is not before me. In him I see but the parable—the visible form of sorrow; I can not taste its fruit. Shall I judge of thy providence without knowing the case? Shall I say thou art stern, cruel, severe, when the facts are not before me? Nay, I shall go to the one object of my knowledge—my own soul. My soul is within my experience, and I would be alone with it and with thee. I can not read the plan of this big world, but I can read the plan of my own life. My sorrows are a mystery to my brother as his are to me, but each of us in his heart has the mystery made manifest. My heart indicates the dark places of thy providence. Thou hast revealed the parable in my solitary soul.

203

Out of the darkness I have grown to thee.
Through the night I have come to thee. Over
the waves I have been borne to thee. From
the grave of buried hopes I have been raised
to thee. I will not be afraid tho the earth be
removed and the hills be shaken with the
swelling seas, for thou hast taught me in the
lone silence of my spirit the exposition of the
great parable—the ark in the flood.

Strength for the Hour

[As thy days, so shall thy strength be.—Deut. 33 : 25.]

My soul, why art thou perplexed about the
future? Seest thou clouds in to-morrow's sky
which thy present strength is inadequate to
meet? God has not given thee thy present
strength to meet the future, but to meet the
present. When thy morrow shall become thy
day thou shalt learn thy power over it. Why
art thou distrest about the unborn sorrow?
Thou thyself art born anew for each new day.
Thine armor is freshly burnished to fight each
rising sun. In the hour of battle thou wilt
laugh at the memory of thy fears. Thou wilt
say even of the last enemy that shall be
conquered—"Oh, death! where is thy sting?
Oh, grave! where is thy victory?" Thou shalt
marvel at thyself when thou passest through
the valley; thou shalt tread it so lightly, so
easily. Thou shalt ask, "Can this be death?"

Thou shalt wonder to hear its desert break into singing, to see its wilderness blossom like the rose. Thou shalt be surprized to find so many lights gleaming in the valley. But the lights will be not in the valley but in thee. God will illuminate thee for the dark day, and what shadows shall abide the blaze of his illumination? The light will not come till the shades come. Weaken not thy spirit by forebodings before battle, for in a moment, in the twinkling of an eye, when the battle-trump shall sound, thy power shall be raised incorruptible, and "as thy days, so shall thy strength be."

A Thirst For God

[Blessed are they which do hunger and thirst after righteousness : for they shall be filled.——Matt. 5 : 6.]

What a wonderful breadth of divine charity! He who is altogether righteous will accept from us even the thirst after righteousness. He will not reserve his blessing until I become actually pure; he will bless my very effort after purity. He will accept the mere desire of him; the mere wish of my heart to be like him; the mere throb of my pulse to be near him. Tho I have not reached him, if only I see in him a beauty that I long for, he will count it unto me for righteousness. Tho I claim not to be like him, and despair

205

ever to touch the hem of his garment, i
only I can admire afar off the kingliness o
his beauty, he will bless my very hunger an
my very thirst for him. Yet, say not, Ol
my soul, that thou hast salvation without
goodness. Thou couldst not hunger after him,
thou couldst not thirst for him, if he were not
already in thee. Thou couldst not see in him
any beauty to desire if thou thyself hadst not
the germ of the same beauty. "We shall be
like him, for we shall see him as he is"; thy
vision of him is the proof of thy likeness to
him. If thou were not like him, thou wouldst
not see him as he is. If he were not in thee,
thou couldst not wish to imitate him—couldst
not even feel thy despair of imitating him.
Thou canst not admire what is out of thy nature, nor seek what is not kindred to thy being. Therefore, my soul, thy hunger pleads
for thee, thy thirst intercedes for thee, thy
longing advocates for thee, thy very sense of
moral want predicts that the spirit is at the
door. Thou canst cry for outward food before thou knowest the taste thereof, but thou
canst not cry for righteousness until thou hast
"tasted that the Lord is good." He who sees
the King in his beauty has himself begun to
be beautiful; he who hungers and thirsts after righteousness is already beginning to be
filled.

George Matheson

The Fire of Love

[Behold, the bush burned with fire, and the bush was not consumed.—Ex. 3 : 2.]

The only thing which is not consumed by burning is my soul. Fire is the death of my body, but fire is the life of my soul. When my goods are burned they perish, but when my soul takes fire it for the first time begins to live. It is the want of fire that consumes my soul. It is because I have so little enthusiasm that I have so little life. The worm of worldly care gnaws at my heart just because there is no fire in my heart to destroy it. My force is wasted by its expenditure on myself. I want something to lift me out of myself in order that I may be strong. Nothing can lift me out of myself but fire, the fire of the heart —love. If I could only be kindled into love, the last enemy would be conquered—death. Love would consume all my cares, but it would give new strength to me. There might be a wilderness around me, but my bush would be glorious—luminous. It would be seen afar off by all the travelers in the desert. It would be a light to lighten the ages, untouched by passing clouds, undimmed by flying years. My heart would never be consumed if only it could burn.

In thee, O Lord, let my heart be kindled! Thy love alone can wake my love. Thy fire alone can impart fire to me. Thy light alone can illuminate and warm me with that ardor which consumes not. Thou divine love of Bethlehem, of Gethsemane, of Calvary, descend into my heart and kindle it! Fan it into thine own sacred flame. Wake it into the fervor of burning zeal. Stir it into the glow of warm aspiration. Stimulate it into the blaze of an high enthusiasm which shall people the very wilderness with interests innumerable. Then shall my heart be ever young. Every hour shall be morning, every season shall be spring, every year shall be the year of jubilee. They that are planted in the house of the Lord shall bring forth fruit even in old age. Their eye shall not be dim, nor their natural strength abated, for the fire that burns within them is a fire that does not consume.

A Golden Evening

[They shall bring forth fruit in old age.—Ps. 92 : 14.]

The fruits of the spiritual life last all the year. Each season has its own appropriate produce. Childhood has its trust, and youth has its hope, and manhood has its work, and old age has its mellow love. They tell me that in old age the night cometh when no man can

George Matheson

work; it is true, but there is no cause for sorrow in it. Every season should have its own fruit, and work is not the fruit of old age. Would you call the summer a time of gloom because it can not give you the primrose? Nay; for its fruit is not the primrose, but the rose full-blown. Shall you call old age a time of gloom because it can not give you work? Nay; for its fruit is not work, but mellowness. The fruits of age belong to itself alone; no other season can bear them. I hear men speak of the decline of life as a time when the powers decay. Well, there are powers that decay, but there are powers that are then only born. There are voices in the soul which wake into music only when the world's voices are silent; there are songs which can be sung only in the night. I have no pure retrospect of love until I have breathed the autumn air, have seen the ingathering of what life has done for me. Prophecies and tongues may fail before the portals of old age, but love will there only reach its perfect glow. Is it not written of the aged Jacob that he "worshiped leaning on the point of his staff''; the sacred fire was strong just where the outer candle was burning low.

Even so, my soul, shall it be with thee. Thy flesh may faint and fail, but thy God is the strength of thy heart. There shall be light at thy evening-time—light which even the morning could not give. Thy youth may faint and grow weary, and thy human strength may utterly fail, but thy faith shall mount up with wings as eagles, and thine inward man shall be renewed day by day. Thy tree of life shall be green when the world's leaves are falling; thou shalt bring forth fruit in old age.

The Power to See God In Sorrow

[Behold, he cometh with clouds; and every eye shall see him.—Rev. 1:7.]

A strange thought, surely; why should every eye see him when he cometh with clouds? Do not the clouds obscure the sight? Would we not have expected the words to be: "Behold he cometh without clouds, and every eye shall see him? Yet bethink thee. It is not said that he cometh in clouds, but he cometh with clouds. The clouds are not to envelop him; they are to accompany him. All the mysteries of life are to follow in his train to prove that they have been all along the servants and ministers of his love. Why is it that to me the God of the universe often seems to hide his face? It is because the clouds of the universe are seen apart from him. They are looked at as blots in his handwriting. They are seen as accidents that have marred the plan of his providence. They are felt as influences that have disputed the reign of his empire. But if I could be told that the clouds are with him, if I could be made to feel that they are parts of himself, modes of his being, features of his plan, workings of his love—if I could be brought to know that, so far from delaying his coming, they are the very chariots in which he comes—then, indeed, I should understand what the seer of Patmos meant. Every eye sees the clouds of life, therefore every eye shall see him when he is known to be coming with the clouds. All hearts have the revelation of sorrow, therefore all hearts shall have a revelation of him when sorrow is known to be a voice from him. O thou that hast made the cloud as well as the sunshine, help me to see that the cloud as well as the sunshine follows in thy train! Help me to learn that thou makest the very winds thy ministering spirits! Help me to know that the affliction of time is actually working out the weight of glory in eternity! Let my vision of thy faithfulness reach even unto the clouds of my earthly day! Show me thy love in the things I called loveless; show me thy face as it shines behind the veil!

Communion With God's Spirit

[I was in the Spirit on the Lord's day.—Rev. 1 : 10.]

No day will help thee, if thou art not in the spirit of the day. No outward thing however beautiful would give thee of itself the sense of beauty. There might be spread before thee the most gorgeous scene on which the eye ever gazed, and there might be given thee the keenest eye that ever gazed on scene; but if thou hadst not the sympathy in thy soul it would be all in vain. How often has the day been bright above thee, and yet has failed to give thee a sense of its joy? When the heart is preoccupied with sorrow, the beauty of nature is not beautiful; it is almost an offense. It is hard that the sun should shine so bright when thou art bereft and weary. It is hard that the bird should sing when thy heart is weeping. It is hard that the roses should bloom when thy life is withered. So hast thou ofttimes felt, oh, my soul. A mere day will not help thee—not even a Lord's day. The holiest Sabbath rest will be nothing to thee if thou hast not rest within. What to thee are the memorial songs of resurrection if thine own spirit be dead? What to thee are the prayers of the assembled throng if thou hast ceased to feel that there is aught worth desiring? What to thee is the stillness of the outward calm if it is but thy leisure hour for inward strife?

Spirit of the day, spirit of the Lord's day, come into my heart and life! Bring down the sunshine and the calm and the worship. Bring down the joy of self-forgetfulness that I may learn the blessedness of thanksgiving. Bring down the resurrection life that I may take up the resurrection song. Make me a Sabbath within that I may behold its mirror without; then shall my days be in spirit the days of the Lord.

Enlargement In Sorrow

[Thou hast enlarged me when I was in distress.—Ps. 4 : 1.]

This is one of the grandest testimonies ever given by man to the moral government of God. It is not a man's thanksgiving that he has been set free from suffering. It is a thanksgiving that he has been set free through suffering: "Thou hast enlarged me when I was in distress." He declares the sorrows of life to have been themselves the source of life's enlargment. And have not you and I a thousand times felt this to be true? It is written of Joseph in the dungeon that "the iron entered into his soul." We all feel that what Joseph needed for his soul was just the iron. He had seen only the glitter of the gold. He had been rejoicing in youthful dreams; and dreaming hardens the heart. He who sheds tears over a romance will not be most apt to help reality; a real sorrow will be too unpoetic for him. We need the iron to enlarge our nature. The gold is but a vision; the iron is an experience. The chain which unites me to humanity must be an iron chain. That touch of nature which makes the world akin is not joy, but sorrow; gold is partial, but iron is universal.

My soul, if thou wouldst be enlarged into human sympathy, thou must be narrowed into the limits of human suffering; Joseph's dungeon is the road to Joseph's throne. Thou canst not lift the iron load of thy brother if the iron hath not entered into thee. It is thy limit that is thine enlargement. It is the shadows of thy life that are the real fulfilment of thy dreams of glory. Murmur not at the shadows; they are better revelations than thy dreams. Say not that the shades of the prison-house have fettered thee; thy fetters are wings—wings of flight into the bosom of humanity. The door of thy prison-house is a door into the heart of the universe. God has enlarged thee by the binding of sorrow's chain.

George Matheson

The Consecration of Our Home Life

[By faith Noah prepared an ark to the saving of his house.—Heb. 11 : 7.]

What a humble, what a modest sphere for the exercise of faith! One would have said that the purpose was quite disproportionate to the work. The ark was a great undertaking, but what was it undertaken for? To save his own family. Is so narrow a sphere worthy to be the object of faith? Is so commonplace a scene as the life of the family circle fit to be a temple for the service of God? I always thought that the family was a secular thing. I always held that the duties of a man's household had nothing to do with his religious duties; that they were far too small things to have a place beside the reading of chapters and the singing of psalms. Going to church was the service of God, but to perform the duties of the household was only the service of man. Here is a voice which tells me all this was a delusion and a dream. Noah is bidden to prepare an ark for the saving of his house. His whole life on earth is a work for his family, and that is counted to him for a religion; it is called faith. He is only allowed to have one motive for action—a domestic motive, a commonplace motive, an intensely practical motive—the protection of his family, the sustenance of his sons and daughters; but because he fills that sphere to the measure of his power, he is reckoned among the company of those who through faith and patience inherited the promise.

My soul, when thou hast finished thy prayers and ended thy meditations, do not say that thou hast left the house of God. If thou art true to thyself thou shalt seek, like the psalmist, never to leave God's house, but to remain in it all the days of thy life. God's house shall to thee be everywhere, and thine own house shall be a part of it. When thou enterest into thy home thou shalt feel that thou art going into a temple, a place of divine worship, an atmosphere of holy service. Thou shalt feel that all the duties of this place are consecrated, that it is none other than the house of God and one of the gates to heaven. Thou shalt feel that every one of its duties is an act of high communion. If thou art breaking thy bread to the family circle thou art fulfilling one form of the command: "this do in remembrance of me." If thou art shedding the warmth of thy love around the domestic hearth, thou art giving to the members of thy household, it may be, their first sense of God. How shall they love the divine Father except through the image of a human fatherhood? How shall they prize the divine Brother except through the form of a human brotherhood? How shall they appreciate the revelation of the house with many mansions if their experience of an earthly home has not been suggestive of peace? Therefore be it thine to make thy house his house. Be it thine to consecrate each word and look and deed in the social life of home. Be it thine to build thine ark of refuge for the wants of common day; verily, thy labor of love shall be called an act of faith.

Divine Trust In Worldly Business

[He went out not knowing whither he went.—Heb. 11 : 8.]

These words are spoken of the call of Abraham—his call to the secular work of founding a nation. It is a great mistake to think that faith is needed only for religious matters. I can not take without it one step in life. Think you that Abraham is an exception to the rule of humanity? He is but the illustration of its rule. To all youth as to his youth there comes at one time a call. My aspirations are the call of God to my soul. There are times when God takes me as he took Abraham out into the clear expanse and points me to the stars of heaven, and says: thou art greater than these, fulfil thy destiny! But then, unlike Abraham, I am not satisfied with God's call; I want proof. I am struck with terror by the arduousness of the way that lies before me. I intend with all my heart to go out on my mission of life, but I find such joy in dreaming about it that I would rather postpone the reality. I say: I will go to-morrow, and the morrow of my going never comes. If youth could only act out its dreams it would soon reach its promised land. But youth does not trust its own aspirings; it is half ashamed of them, it thinks them too good news to be true. It is unwilling to begin the journey of life by the light of faith alone. It feels strength enough for to-day, but not for to-morrow, and therefore it will not go on. How is it to get past that big cloud in to-morrow's sky? How is it to overleap that barrier in the middle of the coming week? How is it to surmount that obstacle on the threshold of the next year? Can faith tell it that?

No; or it would not be faith. Faith never reveals the how; it leaves that for sight to do. Faith points on to the end of the process; it is for reason to show the means. My soul, thou shalt never learn the hidden strength of to-morrow until thou hast used the strength of to-day. It is only by going out without knowing the whither that the whither itself shall be revealed to thee. There is a reserve power sleeping in thy heart and waiting for the moment of need. Go out to meet the moment and the power shall come! Go out in faith, believing in the unseen door that shall unbar at thy approach to let thee through! Go out undaunted by the coming vision of Mount Moriah's sacrifice! Verily, when thou reachest it thou shalt find what now thou seest not—that God himself hath provided for thy sacrificial hour!

A Prayer of Nicholas Ridley

O heavenly Father, the Father of all wisdom, understanding, and true strength, I beseech thee, look mercifully upon me, and send thy Holy Spirit into my breast; that when I must join to fight in the field for the glory of thy holy name, then I, being strengthened with the defense of thy right hand, may manfully stand in the confession of thy faith and of thy truth, and continue in the same unto the end of my life, through our Lord Jesus Christ. AMEN.

A Prayer For Women Who Toil

O God, we pray thee for our sisters who are leaving the ancient shelter of the home to earn their wage in the factory and the store amid the press of modern life. Save them from the strain of unremitting toil that would unfit them for the holy duties of home and motherhood which the future may lay upon them. Give them grace to cherish under the new surroundings the old sweetness and gentleness of womanhood, and in the rough mingling of life to keep their hearts pure and their lives untarnished. Save them from the terrors of utter want. Teach them to stand loyally by their sisters, that by united action they may better their common lot.

If it must be so that our women toil like men, help us still to reverence in them the mothers of the future. But make us determined to shield them from unequal burdens, that the women of our nation be not drained of strength and hope for the enrichment of a few, lest our homes grow poor in the wifely sweetness and motherly love which have been the saving strength and glory of our country. To such as yearn for the love and sovereign freedom of their own home, grant in due time the fulfilment of their sweet desires. By Mary, the beloved, who bore the world's re-

demption in her bosom; by the memory of
our own dear mothers who kissed our souls
awake; by the little daughters who must soon
go out into that world which we are now fash-
ioning for others, we beseech thee that we
may deal aright by all women.

[From "Prayers of the Social Awakening," by Professor
Walter Rauschenbusch, published by the Pilgrim Press;
by permission of author and publisher.]

The Student's Prayer

God, our Salvation and Redemption, who
hast given us nature, grant to us also grace.
Show forth thy light to us, as we grope after
thee, and seek thee, in the shades of ignorance.
Recall us from our errors. Stretch out thy
right hand to us weak ones who can not, with
out thee, attain to thee. Show thy very self to
those who seek nothing besides thee! Break
the clouds of vain phantasies which suffer not
the eye of the mind to behold thee after that
fashion in which thou permittest thyself, the
invisible, to be seen of them who seek thy face,
which is their rest, their goal, beyond which
they crave for nothing seeing that there is
naught beyond the supreme good that is above
all sense.

JOHN SCOTUS ERIGENA

Devotional Classics

Prayer For Easter Day

Almighty and most merciful Father, who hast created and preserved me, have pity on my weakness and corruption. Deliver me from habitual wickedness and idleness; enable me to purify my thoughts, to use the faculties which thou hast given me with honest diligence, and to regulate my life by thy holy Word.

Grant me, O Lord, good purposes and steady resolutions, that I may repent my sins and amend my life. Deliver me from the distresses of vain terror, and enable me, by thy grace, to will and to do what may please thee; that when I shall be called away from this present state, I may obtain everlasting happiness, through Jesus Christ our Lord. AMEN.

SAMUEL JOHNSON

Prayer For the New Year

Our Father, as we enter upon the borders of another year, we come to thee that our consciousness of immortal life may be quickened and renewed. We would not enter upon these untried days with faltering step and fearful heart. May we look into thy face with the child's confidence and joy, saying, "all things

are ours, things present and things to come."
Hold us, our Father, enfolded in thine own
eternity, that we may look out with calmness
upon the flight of time and the mutability of
all earthly things. From this central peace
may we discern with clear vision all the values
of earth and time. May we be kept from
foolish affection for things unworthy of thy
children. May the duties which await us be
done with perfect truth of thought and deed.
May responsibilities be taken with strong
heart and cheerful confidence. If sorrows
await us in the coming days, may we step fearlessly into the gloom, knowing it is but the
shadow of thy outstretched hand of love. We
would share our joys with thee and bear with
simplicity the prosperities of life. Keep us,
we pray thee, in close and living oneness with
thyself and with thy children on all the face
of the earth. May no child of thine ever seem
to us common or unclean. May every service
even to the least of thy little ones be touched
with the grace and tenderness of thy beloved
Son. Let us not forget that he tasted death
for love of men. May we follow him in every
relation and service of our daily life that, like
him, we may hear thy voice speaking also of
us: "this is my beloved son in whom I am
well pleased." We ask it in his name who
was Son of God and Son of man. AMEN.

Prayer For the Nation

Our Father, we rejoice in the great souls whom thou has given to us as a people. Thou hast apportioned to us a great land, a goodly heritage, among the nations of the earth. We have entered upon our inheritance and possest it. But more than all the treasures of the sea and of the land, thou hast enriched us by noble lives, by men of clear vision, of high courage, of stedfast devotion to freedom and justice and truth. We thank thee for all who have loved righteousness better than life; for those who have counted nothing dear to them when the rights of their fellow men have been invaded. For all the lovers and seers and martyrs of liberty and peace and good will among men, we give thee thanks. Forbid, our Father, that the vision which enlightened and kindled their hearts should ever grow dim to our eyes. Forbid that the strait and narrow path which they trod should ever seem too hard for us, and we turn aside into byways of ease and self-seeking. Touch our eyes, we pray thee, to behold the glory and the strength of thy prophets while they are yet alive, that we may take their words as accents of thine own Spirit, that we may follow in their footsteps with joyful obedience. Deliver us, our Father, from the folly of the nations which have loved riches and luxury and the transient glory of power. Save us from that blindness and madness of the peoples who rest on force for safety, and take the sword for selfish and aggressive purposes. Help us to believe in the sufficiency and eternity of righteousness. May we follow with believing hearts and victorious spirits Jesus Christ whom thou hast given, who is this day going forth among the nations, conquering and to conquer, by the might of his goodness and truth and the beauty of his holiness. In his name. AMEN.

JAMES H. ECOB

Index to the Ten Volumes

Roman numerals indicate volumes; Arabic, indicate pages

Index

228

Index

Index

Index

231

Index

Index

233

Index

234

Index

235

Index

236

Index

237

Index

Index

239

Index

Index

241

Index

Index

Index

244

Index

245

Index

246

Index

247

Index

Index

Index

250

Index

251

Index

252

Index

253

Index

Index

255